Mission-Critical Java™ Project Management

Business Strategies, Applications, and Development

Gregory C. Dennis and James R. Rubin

Addison-Wesley

An imprint of Addison Wesley Longman, Inc.

Reading, Massachusetts • Harlow, England • Menlo Park,
California • Berkeley, California • Don Mills, Ontario •
Sydney • Bonn • Amsterdam • Tokyo • Mexico City

The publisher offers discounts on this book when ordered in quantity for special sales. For more information, please contact:

Corporate, Government, and Special Sales
Addison Wesley Longman, Inc.
One Jacob Way
Reading, Massachusetts 01867
(781) 944-3700

Library of Congress Cataloging-in-Publication Data

Dennis, Gregory C. 1965–
    Mission-critical Java™ project management: business strategies, applications, and development / Gregory C. Dennis and James R. Rubin.
        p.   cm.
    Includes index.
    ISBN 0-201-32573-X
    1. Java (Computer program language) 2. Business enterprises—Computer network resources. 3. Web sites. 4. Internet programming. I. Rubin, James R., 1968– . II. Title.
    650′.0285′52762—dc21   98-8514
                                                                                CIP

Chapter opener art, "World Trade Center at Sunrise—NYC," copyright © Ross M. Horowitz / The Image Bank 1999.

ISBN 0-201-32573-X
Text printed on recycled and acid-free paper.
1 2 3 4 5 6 7 8 9 10—MA—0201009998
First Printing August, 1998

This book is a comprehensive guide for managers exploring deployment of Java platform–based business systems. The authors touch on the real-world problems that businesses face and demonstrate how Java technologies help resolve them. The book also spotlights new opportunities that enterprise-wide deployment of the Java platform brings to businesses. Gregory Dennis and James Rubin have put together an excellent resource for managers interested in deploying the Java platform in the enterprise.

> —Alan Baratz
> President, JavaSoft
> A Division of Sun Microsystems, Inc.

Contents

CHAPTER 10   IS JAVA RIGHT FOR EVERYONE?   91

CHAPTER 11   BRIDGING PROCEDURAL AND OBJECT-ORIENTED STYLES   99

CHAPTER 14   OVERCOMING PERFORMANCE CHALLENGES   143

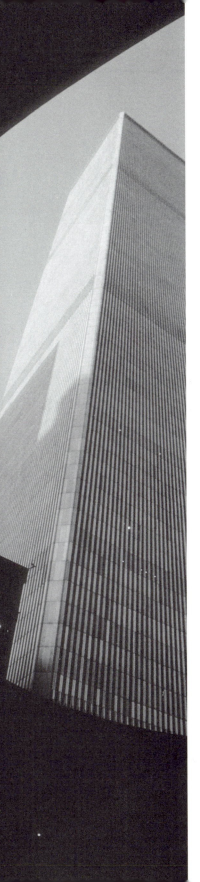

Preface

This book reflects the authors' personal experiences in building the technology infrastructure for *via* World Network, an Andersen Consulting Enterprise. *via* World Network is permanently removing cost and complexity from travel product distribution by connecting corporations and their travelers directly to their preferred suppliers.

Andersen Consulting Enterprises are companies wholly or majority-owned by Andersen Consulting that deliver unique network-centric solutions to changing industries. They exploit advances in network computing to allow companies and industries to acquire or distribute information-based, digital products and services through virtual channels.

As part of Andersen Consulting's Enterprise Group, we have had the opportunity to leverage the knowledge gained in *via* World Network to support additional ventures. Some of these experiences are explored in the other cases presented in this book.

For an overview and outline of the book's purpose and scope, see Chapter 1, which presents a summary of the book and a synopsis of each chapter.

Acknowledgments

The authors would like to express our thanks for the outstanding contributions of all those people who have helped make this book possible. Most importantly, we appreciate the patient and important contributions of our wives, Victoria Dennis and Laura Rubin. The following people were instrumental in reviewing or providing input to the book:

Elmer Baldwin, *via* World Network
Ann Cloos, Andersen Consulting
Michael Dickoff, Andersen Consulting

Richard Erickson, Sun Microsystems
Christopher Gardner, Andersen Consulting
Hal Ghering, Andersen Consulting
Mark Goodyear, Andersen Consulting
Thomas Grudnowski, Andersen Consulting
Mike Hendrickson, Addison Wesley Longman
Regina Hoffman, Andersen Consulting
Capers Jones, author and consultant
Cliff Jury, Andersen Consulting
Phyllis Kennedy, Andersen Consulting
Cynthia Monroe, Andersen Consulting
Mary O'Brien, Addison Wesley Longman
Dr. Judith Simon, University of Memphis
Mike Swenson, Andersen Consulting
Shari Wenker, Andersen Consulting

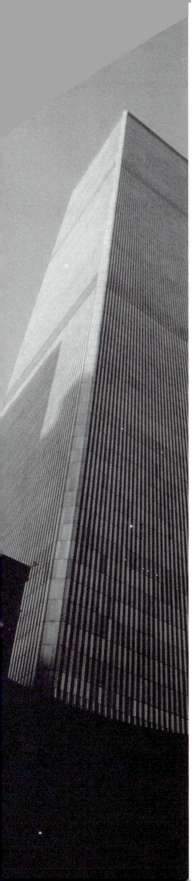

CHAPTER ONE

Building Business Systems

1.1   The Increasing Pace of Competition

The business world has changed rapidly during the 1990s. The pace of competition has increased along with demands to serve customers better. Corporations that do not anticipate new threats to old lines of business or traditional customer segments may see their market positions rapidly eroding in a new era of competition. Customer loyalty and retention are more and more based on the quality of customer service, because the cost of switching from one supplier/provider to another has been dramatically reduced in many industries.

One of the forces that has contributed to the business climate of the 1990s is the pace of competition based on technology. The emergence and rapid adoption of the Internet and electronic commerce by many companies have promoted new ways of reaching customers, suppliers, and business partners. Through the use of these rapidly evolving technologies, barriers to entry are eliminated, costs are reduced, and customer service is improved. In many cases, these improvements result in substantial reductions in the time required to develop a product or service, which in turn increases the competitive pressure felt by many companies. Overall, corporations are faced with a range of competitive threats, including:

- *Existing competitors forming new relationships with customers.* Companies such as overnight delivery, catalog, and airline companies are using the Internet to reach new customers and provide new forms of customer service.

• *Rapid rise of new competitors unconstrained by the old barriers to entry.* Companies selling wine, books, and software are turning to the exclusive use of the Internet to distribute products. These companies have lower marketing and sales costs when compared to traditional approaches of regional warehouses, retail distribution channels, and local marketing campaigns.

The pace of computing technology change has also become a defining force during the 1990s. Corporations responding to competitive threats or developing threats of their own are faced with an increasing array of technology options in delivering new business systems. Along with more options also come more pitfalls and missteps in choosing the wrong technology or in choosing the right technology but at the wrong time. These risks grow in significance to the company as responses to competitive threats become increasingly dependent on computing technology. Choosing the wrong technology may lead a company to develop a business solution that works in the laboratory but does not work well as a foundation for a mission-critical business system.

This book addresses the advantages gained and challenges faced by companies in responding to competitive threats by leveraging the Java technology created by Sun Microsystems. Java technology has enjoyed a rapid rise in popularity through its close association with the rise in usage and adoption of the Internet. Java technology's status as a programming language for the Internet has given it broad exposure in both the technology and the business press. The capabilities and features of Java computing provide compelling benefits in building business systems; however, as in all new technologies, there are challenges to overcome.

This book is a guide for managers in leveraging Java computing. Through real-life case examples and in-depth subjects (security, performance, productivity), it addresses the advantages, challenges, and issues facing companies in the use of Java technology for deploying real-world, mission-critical business systems. Java computing is demonstrated to be a powerful tool for business and technology managers. In addition, insights into the issues and challenges in the use of Java technology, and strategies for overcoming these hurdles, are provided. This book serves business and technology managers in their efforts to:

- Map corporate technology strategy

- Develop new business systems with Java technology

- Lead business application developers in their use of Java technology

1.2 Java Technology's Rapid Rise

Java technology has had a tremendous impact on the computing world since its 1.0 release in 1996. Java technology has been strongly endorsed by major computing products/services corporations, has captured the interest and attention of programmers around the world, and has received a tremendous amount of media attention. This attention is due in large part to computing advancements Java technology provides, including the ability to support:

- Platform-independent applications

- Dynamically downloaded and installed applications requiring no user assistance

- Secure application download through unsecure networks (the Internet, for example)

- Improved application quality over C/C++ development through a simpler programming language and improved error handling

Java technology's dramatic rise in popularity has been closely tied to the growth of and interest in the Internet and, more specifically, the World Wide Web (the Web). Media, industry, and even popular attention tracked the rapid evolution of the Web during the mid-1990s. The Web became entrenched in popular culture as media advertisements referenced corporate and product Web pages, and personal Web pages became a way for people to express themselves, look for jobs, or find other people with similar interests.

The announcement and early release of Java technology in 1995 occurred during the early days of the Web's adoption by the business community. The Java programming language was demonstrated to the world as a powerful new technology that enlivened Web pages with animation and interactive content. Web pages were based solely on a language called HyperText Markup Language (HTML), which is a scripting language that provides a browser with static instructions about a Web page's format and composition. Java improved the interactive nature of the Web page by allowing developers to create dynamic applications that immediately responded to user requests without having to make relatively slow requests through the Internet.

This capability was being hailed and rapidly adopted as Sun Microsystems made a free Java Development Kit (JDK) available over the Internet. Soon, thousands of developers were creating dynamic content on Web pages and Java was envisioned to have a major impact on the computing industry by both the technology press and the general business press.

Java technology has a number of other features and capabilities that will ensure its success beyond mere animated Web pages. Many of these features come from Java technology's heritage. Java technology's direct predecessor was an effort by Sun Microsystems to create a programming language that would operate within the limited memory and complex application requirements of interactive television. The resulting technology addressed the challenges of multiple platforms, dynamic application download, memory management, and improved application quality.

It is in many of these areas that Java technology represents an opportunity to make dramatic improvements in the quality, longevity, and cost of business systems, but its impact goes beyond improvements in application programming languages. Java technology's impact extends from corporate strategy to business systems deployment to application developers because it is an enabling technology, simplifies and improves the deployment of business applications, and improves the productivity of application developers. Although the use of Java technology is not without challenges, these hurdles can be managed and overcome.

1.3   Why a Book?

This book is based on the authors' involvement in leading the development and deployment of business applications based on Java technology. These experiences occurred between mid-1995 and mid-1997 and were based in large part on the initial release of services by *via* World Network, an Andersen Consulting enterprise. This new company made a strategic decision in early 1996 to leverage Java as the base technology for the complex travel management products it would produce. The successful implementation of the *via* World Network system formed the base of skills used to develop additional business systems discussed in this book. With the early 1997 2.0 release of *via* World Network, the application measured more than 15,000 function points in size and had more than 800,000 lines of Java code.

This book explores the significant benefits and hurdles associated with leveraging of Java technology for business applications. The experiences from two years of intensive Java application development resulted in the learning of several lessons. It is the authors' intention to convey these lessons in corporate technology strategy, complex system development, and application developer impacts in a way that reduces the risk and challenge of leveraging Java computing for business systems.

There are many reasons to use Java technology for business application development. Based on the case studies documented in this book, a few of the compelling benefits Java technology has demonstrated are:

- Use of platform independence to reduce computing platform costs by 50 percent

- Application development productivity gains of 10 to 20 percent

- Approximately 75 percent fewer application errors in newly released production applications

Achieving these benefits was accomplished only by overcoming significant obstacles. From the relative volatility of a new technology to slow performance to a lack of development tools, there are significant challenges to using Java technology and achieving the benefits outlined above.

Where possible, the authors have attempted to document quantitatively the benefits and challenges associated with Java computing. The quantitative comparisons are based on documented results of C, C++, and COBOL application development and operation. Owing to tight timelines and a limited budget for monitoring and tracking system development, not all of the authors' conclusions are based on quantitative data and are qualitative in nature. These qualitative conclusions will be apparent to the reader and are based on decades of experience by the authors in developing, deploying, and operating business applications.

This book is best used as a guide and primer for business and technology managers considering the use of Java computing for business applications. It provides experienced-based insights that give the manager a head start in developing a Java-based business application; however, this book is not a cookbook that predicts the results of every business application development project. Business application development projects are significantly impacted by the culture of the company, the skillset of the developers, and the maturity of the technologies selected. Use this book to prepare and plan, but not as a substitute for strong and active project management. Every application development project must be managed according to the people involved, the circumstances experienced, and the business requirements at hand.

1.4 General Overview

This book is a manager's guide/reference in understanding the benefits and challenges in building Java-based business systems. Both case studies and subject chapters are used to guide the manager. The case studies provide managers with a real-world context and the results/issues of building a Java-based system. The focused subject chapters are stand-alone units that explore specific issues such as application performance and developer productivity. The book has been organized as follows.

- via *World Network case study (Chapter 2)*. Explores the real-world decisions and experiences in building a company's services based on Java technology. Many of the book's insights are based on the successes achieved and challenges faced by *via* World Network in building and maintaining a complex Java-based business system.

- *Additional case studies (Chapter 3 through Chapter 5)*. These case studies provide additional examples of how Java technology has been used to build business systems.

- *Corporate strategy (Chapter 6 through Chapter 10)*. These chapters address the strategic issues in the decision to use Java technology for creating business applications. They explore Java technology's ability to create new business opportunities, its ability to remain a viable technology, and its successes in converting existing business systems. Additional chapters focus on dealing with Java computing as an emerging, not yet mature, technology. A final chapter explores the questions and issues to consider when evaluating Java technology as an appropriate fit for an enterprise's business system.

- *Business systems (Chapter 11 through Chapter 16)*. These chapters address the impacts of Java technology on the development and operation of business applications. A lesson learned in building business systems in Java technology was its ability to bridge procedural and object-oriented development styles and its ability to reduce the cost of developing technical infrastructure for business systems. Additional chapters explore Java technology's use for more than applets (small applications that automatically run within a browser) and its ability to support secure, highly available, and high-performance business systems.

- *Application development (Chapter 17 through Chapter 20)*. These chapters address advantages and challenges associated with the actual construction of

Java-based business systems. Subjects include the importance of developer interest in Java programming, the training of Java developers, and the productivity improvements Java technology can bring to application development. The final chapter explores the impacts of Java technology on existing development tools and processes.

1.5 Case Study Chapters

Four case studies provide examples of Java technology's viability as a platform for building business systems. Each of these case studies follows a consistent approach.

- Background of industry and business problem

- Technology solution for addressing the business problem

- Use of Java technology in the business system

- Summary of the advantages and challenges in using Java technology

1.5.1 *via* World Network (Chapter 2)

via World Network is an Andersen Consulting enterprise that through its services reduces the cost and complexity of travel product distribution. *via* World Network was a pioneer in the use of Java technology for business systems. This case study traces the history of *via* World Network's use of Java technology as the platform for providing its travel management services.

1.5.2 Customer Sales Support (Chapter 3)

A customer sales support system designed to assist sales agents in taking orders and promoting additional sales opportunities is profiled. This system was originally developed within an integrated application development tool and was converted to Java. The challenges and lessons associated with this conversion are discussed in this case study.

1.5.3 Customer Service Support (Chapter 4)

Chapter 4 profiles a document management system designed to support the on-line review of customer bills by customer support representatives. The document management system involves a number of technologies including browsers, imaging, and browser plug-ins. This case study demonstrates the use of Java applets as the critical integrating technology.

1.5.4 Human Resource Service Delivery (Chapter 5)

This chapter profiles the design and construction of a prototype system that coordinated and facilitated the use of access to human resource facilities and information. Java technology served as the basis for the development of Web-based access tools and server-side business logic.

1.6   Subject Chapter Overview

The format of the subject chapters follows a consistent approach.

- The business context of the subject

- Technology challenges and requirements

- Specifics on the use and impacts of Java technology

- A detailed example (where appropriate)

- A summary of the key messages of the chapter

The intent of these chapters is to help business and technical managers understand the advantages and challenges in planning, developing, and deploying Java-based business systems.

1.6.1 An Enabling Technology (Chapter 6)

When Java technology is used to develop business applications, opportunities to reach new customers, reduce costs, and improve the efficiency of systems are made possible. Java applications can be deployed in a variety of styles, allowing the business to tailor a single application to the needs of both centralized and remote users. Java programming is the language of low-cost network computers that can be used to reduce the expense of computing hardware for clerical applications. Through platform independence, Java applications improve the ability of businesses to make hardware price/performance decisions. Java technology's integration of Internet and Web technologies enables businesses more rapidly to adapt and deploy solutions to customers and employees.

1.6.2 Is Java a Fad? (Chapter 7)

Java technology's acceptance has been global, not only geographically but also technologically. Java technology has built a broad base of support, which encourages development of third-party products and solutions such as application development tools and performance tuning aids. As third-party products continue to emerge, business systems are deployed more rapidly because less technology infrastructure must be custom or in-house developed. Java technology's broad acceptance encourages a strong community for support and guidance that reduces the risk and exposure of companies as they begin to work with Java technology.

1.6.3 Converting Existing Business Systems (Chapter 8)

Chapter 8 explores the benefits and challenges of converting existing business systems to Java technology. Although the conversion requires time, money, and a cleanly designed/implemented existing system, the conversion to Java can be accomplished. An example approach to converting an existing system to Java technology is provided.

1.6.4 Managing a New Technology (Chapter 9)

Java technology has become so popular that technology vendors such as Sun Microsystems (the original inventors of Java) are inundated with support requests. As a result of this overwhelming interest in Java technology, it is important to formalize relationships with technology vendors. In addition, Java technology is relatively new, and the skills, support, and infrastructure have not reached the level of a mature technology. An incremental approach to minimizing the support risk in using Java technology is covered in Chapter 9.

1.6.5 Is Java Right for Everyone? (Chapter 10)

Not all companies have the right culture and/or background to leverage Java technology. Java programming is a new and emerging technology, and the use of Java computing requires the ability to be adaptable and flexible as the technology evolves. Companies should carefully consider whether or not Java programming is the right platform for delivery of critical business systems. A strategy for developing the background and skills for building Java-based business systems is included.

1.6.6 Bridging Procedural and Object-Oriented Styles (Chapter 11)

For more than a decade, technology visionaries have lauded the benefits of object computing. Despite these endorsements, object technology has not become an overwhelmingly accepted, routine, or mainstream approach to business systems application development. Object development requires substantial changes in approach and significant investments in training for most businesses. Java technology represents a "bridge" allowing today's business application developers to enter the world of object development without having to make substantial changes in methodology or significant training investments. Chapter 11 provides a strategy for leveraging an existing base of procedural developers in building an object-based system through use of the Java programming language.

1.6.7 Building Execution Architectures (Chapter 12)

Client/server business applications require the construction and operation of complex infrastructures for network communications, concurrent processing, platform independence, and error management. This infrastructure can be broadly termed the execution architecture of a business application. Java technology simplifies and in some cases eliminates the building or buying of complex execution architecture infrastructure.

1.6.8 Moving beyond Applets (Chapter 13)

Java technology can be used to support business applications far more complex than applets downloaded from a Web page. Chapter 13 addresses three challenges in building Java-based client/server applications and presents an example that outlines the key technology components required to build a client/server system. Chapter 13 also discusses the effects of emerging distributed computing standards (CORBA and Active/X) on Java applications.

1.6.9 Overcoming Performance Challenges (Chapter 14)

Although performance is a critical concern for a business application, performance concerns associated with Java applications can be successfully addressed. A performance strategy and example performance improvements are documented. These example performance improvements provide specific areas to review and address when developing a Java-based system.

1.6.10 Making Applications Secure (Chapter 15)

Concerns have also been raised in regard to the Java security model. Chapter 15 provides reasons why for many companies this issue is overstated and also gives insights into building applications that are secure and Internet-friendly.

1.6.11 Building Highly Available Systems (Chapter 16)

Highly available business systems (ones that must run every day and for 24 hours per day) are difficult to build, especially when using client/server technology. Different strategies exist for building highly available systems, but most do not address one of the weakest areas in large business systems—application resilience. Chapter 16 discusses Java technology's effect on the quality of application programs and provides an example of an overall Java-based business system built to be highly available.

1.6.12 Motivating Application Developers (Chapter 17)

Java programming has developed a strong following among developers from around the world, and this popularity can benefit companies building Java applications. Java programming's popularity with business application developers can be associated with improvements in application development.

1.6.13 Learning the Technology (Chapter 18)

The use of Java programming to build business applications requires training of existing and new application developers. The advantages and challenges associated with training developers in Java programming are explored. A sample outline of a training session for Java developers is provided.

1.6.14 Improving Developer Productivity (Chapter 19)

Building of complex business applications involves significant expenses in both cost and time. Features of Java technology allow Java applications to be developed more quickly than comparable C or C++ applications. Metrics regarding Java application development are provided.

1.6.15 New Development Tools and Processes (Chapter 20)

Business application development tools and processes are tied to the programming language used to build the system. While not all tools and processes must change, a significant portion of the existing infrastructure needs to be either modified or replaced when complex Java-based business systems are built.

1.7 Summary

The rapid adoption of electronic commerce technologies has increased the pace of competition in the business environment. Companies must leverage new technologies to remain competitive, but have little time to research the viabilities and effects of these technologies. The popularity of and excitement about Java technology make it a prime target as a platform for developing business systems. Although Java technology's initial and ongoing success has been attributed almost exclusively to its ability to animate World Wide Web pages, significant advantages can be achieved through its ability to simplify and improve the delivery of complex business systems. The Java platform allows businesses to be more effective in meeting customer needs, reducing the cost of delivering applications, and leveraging existing application development technology investments. This book is a collection of cases and insights for guiding business and technical managers in achieving these business benefits. The focus of this book is on identifying challenges in building business systems, providing strategies and potential solutions, and summarizing the key lessons learned.

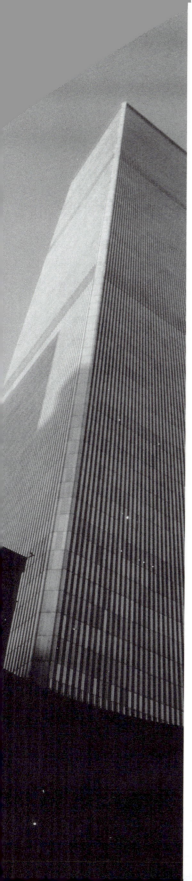

CHAPTER TWO

Case Study: *via* World Network

2.1   Introduction

via World Network is a company that was formed by Andersen Consulting in 1995 to market electronic commerce solutions to the travel industry. The solutions developed by *via* World Network were pioneering in their use of Java technology. This case study explores *via* World Network's business requirements, the decision process behind the selection, and a hindsighted view of the pros and cons of using Java technology.

2.2   Reinventing Travel Product Distribution

During the summer of 1995, a small team set out to explore the feasibility of reengineering the way in which travel planning products were distributed to corporate business travelers. The business case for this project focused on reducing the cost of travel product distribution (more than $20 billion in North American air travel) and improving service to business travelers. This team consisted of ten people who understood business travelers, the travel industry, and client/server technology. The strategy developed by this team required:

- Multiple forms of user interfaces

- A highly available transaction processing engine

- High-speed connections to existing travel inventory systems

Multiple user interfaces were required to meet the demanding requirements of business travelers. Generally, most such travelers and their assistants prefer the ability to plan and prepare for trips from their personal computers. However, these travelers are also the ones who most frequently change their travel plans at the last minute. In these last-minute-change situations (for example, a meeting has run late and the traveler is scrambling to reschedule flights), personal computers are inconvenient to start up and connect into travel systems; however, pay phones and cellular phones are easy to find and convenient to use. Through voice response and voice recognition technologies, travelers would be able to alter their travel plans conveniently and quickly.

Despite the differences between computer and voice interfaces, they both require the same set of core travel product distribution services. This led to a vision of the development of a wide variety of user interfaces including personal digital assistants, self-service kiosks, and televisions, all accessing the same back-end core travel product distribution services (see Figure 2.1).

Reengineering the delivery of travel products rested on the quality and availability of the core services (such as ticket pricing and reservation booking). This core functionality must deliver services at a low cost, with high reliability and consistent performance. In addition, these services must be delivered to a variety of user interfaces including computers and telephones. Existing industry systems offered comparable services with high reliability, but were built with technology

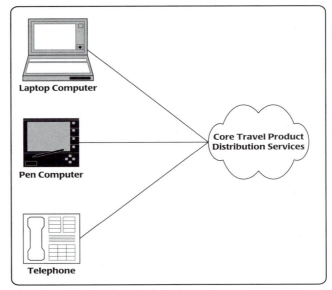

Figure 2.1   Multiple user interfaces

that did not easily support multiple user interfaces, could not securely communicate over unsecure networks (for example, the Internet), and did not support rapid growth of low-cost, high-performance transactions. Based on previous travel industry and client/server operations experience, the decision was made to build and operate the core travel product distribution services on a low-cost, high-performance client/server system.

The *via* World Network system also had to be connected to existing airline inventory systems. These inventory systems were based on IBM mainframe systems using the Transaction Processing Facility (TPF) on-line transaction processing system. These systems were originally built to support users on character-based terminals. Travel agents and airline employees communicate with these systems through cryptic character-based commands that require weeks of training to understand and use. Over the last few years, the inventory systems of suppliers (for example, airlines, hotels, and car rental companies) have worked closely with the large computer reservation systems (for example, Amadeus, Galileo, Sabre, and WorldSpan) to develop more efficient ways of communicating between travel industry inventory systems. These communication requirements led to the emergence of an Electronic Data Interchange (EDI) standard. Unfortunately, neither the cryptic character-based nor the EDI technologies are suited for supplying low-cost, efficient, and convenient travel product distribution for business travelers. The *via* World Network approach would deliver travel services in a manner suitable for business travelers while still interfacing with existing inventory systems (see Figure 2.2) using EDI and character-based communications.

2.3 Risk Management

Given the maturity of Java technology in late 1995, most would consider the decision to build a complex, mission-critical business system in the Java language a risky one. The management of this risk was accomplished through the following evolutionary, step-by-step decision process:

- *Desktop viability.* Proving Java technology as a viable technology for desktop applications

- *Market acceptance.* Demonstrating that the market would accept Java technology as a viable development technology

- *Business case.* Developing a business case for using Java programming as the base software technology

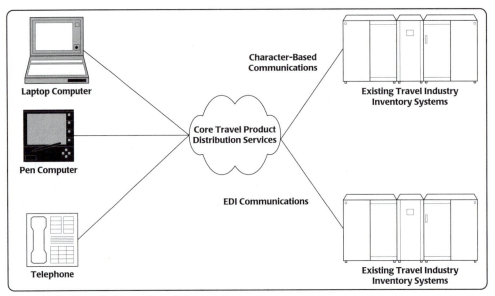

Figure 2.2   Interfacing with existing systems

- *Software (SW) conversion.* Converting existing C software to the Java language

- *Developer training.* Training application developers in the development of Java-based systems

- *Application build.* Designing, developing, testing, and installing a full-scale production business system

Figure 2.3 outlines the project timeline for *via* World Network.

2.3.1 Desktop Viability

As of November 1995, the *via* World Network team had decided on the use of a proven technology for the desktop. Technologies such as C, C++, Visual Basic, and PowerBuilder had been around for more than five years, and successful desktop applications had been delivered on these platforms. Despite Java technology's lack of proven success, its promoted benefits encouraged the *via* World Network team to undertake a low-budget, proof-of-concept exercise to determine its viability as *via* World Network's desktop application technology.

The proof-of-concept exercise demonstrated that the Java language was more than just a language for dynamic World Wide Web applets. The Java language showed itself not only the equal of but superior to traditional languages (C or C++, for example) in areas such as automatic memory management and

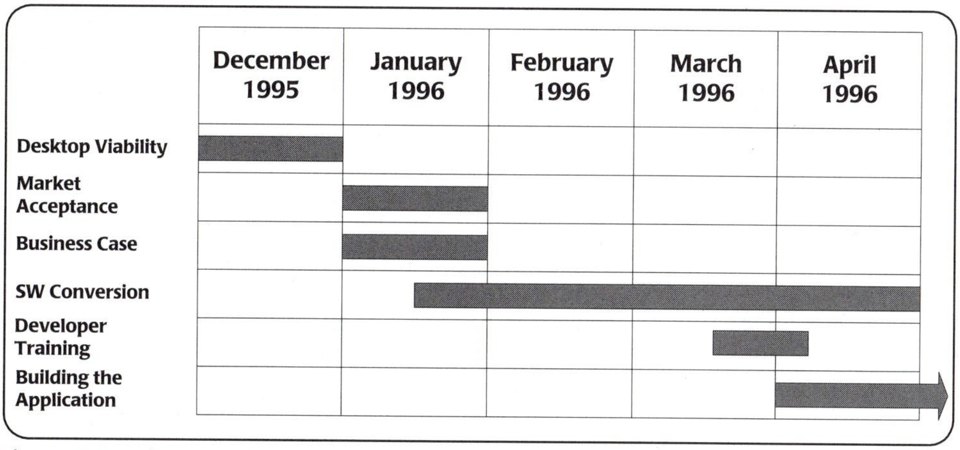

	December 1995	January 1996	February 1996	March 1996	April 1996
Desktop Viability	▓▓▓				
Market Acceptance		▓▓▓			
Business Case		▓▓▓			
SW Conversion		▓▓▓▓▓▓▓▓	▓▓▓▓▓▓▓▓	▓▓▓▓▓▓▓▓	
Developer Training				▓▓▓	
Building the Application					▓▓▓→

Figure 2.3 Risk management timeline

improved multithreading capabilities. While the Java environment did not have all of the development tools of integrated environments such as Visual Basic and PowerBuilder, the Java language provided better functionality for building an Internet-based, client/server system because of its browser integration, platform independence, security features, and dynamic download capabilities. Despite having only C and C++ skills, the two developers on the project were able very quickly to master the language, develop working applications, and become more productive than with C or C++ because of Java's simpler syntax and language constructs.

The result of the exercise was a powerful, if somewhat unrefined, desktop application for travel planning and booking. The application took a total of 300 hours to complete, contained six windows, and was able to demonstrate Java's powerful capabilities.

- *Platform independence.* The application was demonstrated on UNIX and Windows 95.

- *Rapid development.* The application was built within a month despite a lack of traditional tools such as a debugger or graphical user interface painter.

- *Complex, concurrent application execution.* The application demonstrated the ability of the Java technology easily to support simultaneous (or threaded) activity in multiple windows. A user was able to view multiple flight availability windows. Each of these flight availability windows independently updated the appropriate level of seat inventory for the flight.

- *Simple network communication.* The Java language supported easy and robust tools for making and receiving requests over networks, including the Internet.

- *Powerful and compelling multimedia features.* The prototype employed animation and audio to prompt the traveler when making reservations.

- *Dynamic application download.* The demonstration did not need to be installed on a user's machine. As updates were completed, the new version was placed on a single Web site.

2.3.2 Market Acceptance

The proof-of-concept exercise became the basis for a demonstration only one month later in January 1996. This was a crucial demonstration of the technology, because it would determine whether travel industry executives would or would not accept the Java technology as the basis for delivering *via* World Network's services. This exercise was to show key travel industry executives the ability of Java technology to have live, real-time application content delivered through the Web and executed on the desktop.

The demonstration was developed within a month. This demonstration allowed the executives to book a flight through a Java application. During the demonstration, a comparison of the Java application was run against a well-known Web page with similar functionality. The Web page took more time to download its first two pages to the desktop than it took for the Java application to download and fully execute. Even when the Web page was downloaded, it was a static page requiring the user to submit information and wait for a new page to be retrieved over the network, whereas the Java application immediately responded to the user. Examples of "active" responses included the ability to:

- draw a line on a map between the origin and destination cities

- see dynamic seat availability for the fare classes of a flight

The travel industry executives clearly saw that the Java technology was more than "hype" and could be used to deliver applications to customers that would surpass those of their competition. These executives endorsed the project's approach of using the Java technology as an Internet-based desktop application.

2.3.3 Business Case

For *via* World Network, the primary business processing occurs not on the client application (for example, GUI or voice) but in a centralized data center. In the data center, server-side services respond to client requests (see Figure 2.4). Once the Java technology had proved itself on the desktop, the team investigated the use of the Java language for the server-side core business logic. The key test was the language's ability to act as a server and process network requests. This processing had to occur from within a continuously running server and be highly available.

It did not take long to discover that the Java language would be able to support server-based processing. A team member found a Java server available free of charge on the Web. This person downloaded the Java server, learned how to run it, and began testing it. After several hours of stress testing dozens of concurrent clients calling the server, the team not only was convinced that the Java technology could do the job, but also was surprised at the ease with which the Java language could be used to build server-side applications.

Based on the success at proving the technology platform for desktop applications and server-side computing, the Java language was seen as a platform that could be used for development of the entire system. But before the language became the basis for *via* World Network's application development, a business case had to be developed to answer the following questions.

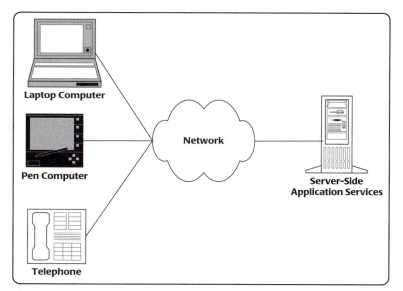

Figure 2.4   User interfaces and server-side services

- *C and COBOL developer productivity.* The project had an existing team of C and COBOL developers. Could C and COBOL (that is, procedural) developers be productive in a Java (or object-oriented) environment?

- *C and COBOL code portability.* The project had more than 50,000 lines of existing C and COBOL applications that had to be leveraged. Could the existing C and COBOL code be converted to the Java language?

- *Cost of a Java execution architecture.* The project already had a development environment and development toolset assuming C/COBOL/Visual Basic/PowerBuilder development. What would be the up-front cost of building an infrastructure to support business process development in the Java language?

- *Training materials and a development environment.* Switching to the Java language would require training. Could training materials and a development environment be prepared in time for application developers?

- *Managing technology risks.* The Java language was a new, unproven technology. What were the technology risks, and how would they be managed?

2.3.3.1 C and COBOL Developer Productivity

The project was able to leverage personnel who had significant skills in C and COBOL but not strong skills in the Java language or even object-oriented programming. This was accomplished by providing a "C-like" environment for programmers while leveraging the object-oriented features of the Java language. The environment created for developers had the following features.

- Business application architects defined and designed business process objects.

- Each business process object was implemented within a "shell." The shell was a project-wide framework that simplified application development by hiding a majority of object-oriented concepts.

- Strict programming standards that made Java programming very similar to programming in C were defined and closely followed.

2.3.3.2 C and COBOL Code Portability

In January 1996, a sample C application was chosen to test the portability of the application from C to Java. After roughly a week, the code had been converted and successfully compiled as a Java application. More importantly, a step-by-step process had been developed to guide the further conversion of the existing C code to Java and to estimate the amount of work required to perform the conversion. More information on this conversion process is presented in Chapter 8.

2.3.3.3 Cost of a Java Execution Architecture

An execution architecture is the part of the business application that performs complex technology functions (database access, communications, etc.). This part of the *via* World Network application did not perform business functions, such as pricing a ticket or reserving inventory, but focused on simplifying and standardizing the application developer's use of facilities such as network communication and database access. The cost to *via* World Network of converting an existing C/C++ execution architecture to the Java language was estimated to be equal to or less than the cost of 1,000 days of effort. Although this represented a significant development expense, it was much less than the cost of the more than 10,000 days spent to create the original execution architecture. In the event that the conversion estimate was inaccurate, a viable but less desirable alternative was to develop Java applications but make use of the language's ability to call C routines. In this scenario, the Java applications would leverage the existing C architecture but would lose their portability across platforms and the system would increase in complexity as a multilanguage implementation with Java-to-C interfaces.

Another reason to convert to the Java language was the requirement of supporting a full-scale on-line transaction processing environment. Because of powerful capabilities in the Java language (that is, concurrent processing and network connectivity), there was a belief that building a Java-based transaction processing infrastructure would take less effort than using a comparable C infrastructure.

2.3.3.4 Training Materials and a Development Environment

Once the environment for application programmers began to look like a C (procedural) project, the training process was simple and easy; creating the development environment was more difficult. The real challenge was not in developing custom tools, procedures, or standards but in leveraging third-party Java debugging and programming tools. The business case expectation was that these third-party tools would quickly emerge; this, however, did not turn out to be the case.

2.3.3.5 Managing Technology Risks

Three major technology risks were identified and addressed.

- *Java application performance might not meet the needs of an on-line transaction processing environment.* This risk was managed by working closely with vendors and by using early identification of performance-critical application routines.

- *The technology might not work as advertised.* The proof-of-concept exercise minimized this risk; however, some features might be discovered in later stages of development. The ability to access existing C routines was believed to be sufficient to manage this risk.

- *The Java technology might wither and die, and alternatives (for example, Microsoft ActiveX) might become the standard for Internet programming.* Microsoft had endorsed the Java language and appeared to be developing a strategy for the coexistence of Java and ActiveX. In addition, Sun Microsystem's release of Java technology at no cost ensured its widespread adoption around the world as the preferred programming language for the Internet.

2.3.4 Software Conversion

During the business case, it was proven that existing code could be converted from C or COBOL to the Java language. A small test of 300 lines of code convinced management that *via* World Network would be able to leverage more than 50,000 lines of existing C and COBOL code if the project used the Java language as the base technology. When development began, one of the first projects was to convert the existing code base. To minimize the cost to the project, *via* World Network leveraged developers with no background in Java by providing them with a clear step-by-step process. After several weeks of work, the complex business logic had been converted successfully. There were a few issues, however.

- *Testing took longer than anticipated.* Whereas the conversion was fairly straightforward and accurately estimated, testing time had been grossly understated. The team was over budget because the modules had to be thoroughly retested. Retesting was required because every line of code in the C and COBOL modules had to be rewritten.

- *The team performed a double conversion for the COBOL code—from COBOL to C and then from C to COBOL.* The fear was that COBOL's syntax was too disparate from Java's syntax, and the team felt that the double conversion would be easier. This double conversion took longer than budgeted and in retrospect was not necessary.

- *The new Java execution architecture to which the team was converting was not completed in time.* This caused the conversion team difficulties in conversion and forced them to make guesses and then retrofit the code once the execution architecture was completed.

Despite these setbacks, the conversion was completed and the converted code eventually made its way into production. Through the use of programmers with little Java programming knowledge and a standard procedure for converting the modules, *via* World Network was able to convert complex business logic from an older, established system to a new system built entirely in the Java language.

2.3.5 Developer Training

The last task to perform before full system development could begin was to turn C- and COBOL-trained developers into Java developers. This was done by leveraging the Java knowledge of a few key individuals. The experienced Java programmers created training materials and gave two two-week training courses to all of the *via* World Network developers and management team members. The training courses addressed the following topics.

- Object-oriented programming

- Technology fundamentals

- Basics of Java programming and exercises

- Advanced Java programming and exercises

- How to develop applications within *via* World Network

- The *via* World Network Java execution architecture

- Java news and trends

With this minimal training, the *via* World Network developers were able to build a large, complex Java application measured at more than 15,000 function points. The development time and effort estimates were based on programming metrics for experienced C developers. In the first six months, the team did not meet these estimates, but in the second six months these estimates were exceeded (refer to Chapter 19 for more information on the productivity of Java developers).

2.4   Building the Application

Within a year, *via* World Network's team of 50 developers had created a large Java application of more than 15,000 function points. The Java language proved to be a robust and full-featured language, because fewer problems than expected were experienced in the development of a transaction processing system. In the final analysis, the Java technology delivered value in the following ways.

- *The Java technology supported the development of a complex, large-scale business process.* Nothing in the Java language prevented application developers from meeting their business processing objectives. In fact, development using the Java language had fewer bugs, and developers created better applications than they could have developed if a language such as C or C++ had been used. A clear example of this occurred during the first release of the *via* World Network system. After building a system of almost 400 function points, the team assembled the entire application for its first end-to-end test. This logic successfully executed on its very first try. The team of former C and C++ developers was surprised to see no evidence of the memory management problems that plague development in C and C++.

- *In general, Java's performance met the needs of the business application.* In much of the application, the performance of the Java logic was acceptable and the focus of tuning was on either complex business logic or the execution architecture built to support business applications. The performance of the application was greatly enhanced by the emergence of Java performance tools, such as runtime compilers, in the fall of 1996. These compilers reduced application runtime by as much as 80 percent in some cases.

- *The technology worked as advertised.* No major bugs in the Java technology were discovered. The Java runtime environment had been very thoroughly tested and was a robust implementation. The biggest technical challenge was in resolving memory allocation problems in C routines called from Java code. These routines had to be built in C to achieve the database access functionality required for this system. So, in effect, the biggest technology challenges were not in the Java implementation but in the C code that was written to access relational databases.

- *Java prospered.* The Java technology did not wither, and a steady base of third-party software development tools emerged from major software developers, including Microsoft. Even though the Java technology is still evolving, it appears that there is enough momentum behind it to establish it as a permanent technology.

- *Java developers were more productive than C developers.* As suspected, training materials were not difficult to create for C developers using the Java language. A more challenging problem was the creation of developer productivity tools such as on-line debuggers. The development of these tools did not occur as fast as the developers had hoped, and they were forced to perform debugging without these tools. While the lack of these tools slowed down developers, the simplicity of the Java language and syntax reduced the need for complex application debugging. Initially, the resulting application developer productivity was slightly less than in previous experience with C-based development efforts. As the development environment matured, Java developers became more productive than their C counterparts. Chapter 19 explores in greater detail the improvements in developer productivity.

- *C and COBOL applications were effectively converted to the Java language.* The *via* World Network team was able to convert tens of thousands of lines of C and COBOL code to the Java language by establishing rigid and predictable standards of conversion.

- *The Java business applications developed were more robust than comparable C versions.* In earlier C-based development efforts, significant time was spent debugging memory allocation and error-handling functions that *via* World Network was able to debug with the Java language. The testing of business process logic did not cause losses in time resulting from the need to fix complex technology bugs or from applications that intermittently suffered memory allocation problems. For the first six months after the first two production releases, *via* World Network experienced 75 percent fewer production defects than would have been expected with a C/C++ system.

2.5 Technology Solution

Through heavy use of the Java technology and a combination of computing technologies, *via* World Network created an end-to-end solution. The following were the key technical components.

- *Java applet.* The user interface consisted of a Java applet executing through a commercially available browser.

- *Internet and intranet access.* The communication capabilities of browsers and Web servers were utilized for communications between the Java applet and network services. Both standard and proprietary encryption/decryption routines were implemented to increase the level of security.

- *Web server.* A commercially available Web server was installed and configured to handle network communication into the *via* World Network data center.

- *Voice recognition/response interface.* Third-party products handling both voice recognition and response were integrated into the system. The voice interface was configured so that it could properly communicate with the same network services used by the Java applets.

- *Server-side services.* A proprietary implementation of a continuously executing process was created to service network requests. The process received a request over the network (from either the voice or GUI interface) and invoked a business component (that is, ticket pricing, seat availability, or booking). After the business component was executed, the results were returned to the requesting interface.

- *Database.* A highly available Relational DataBase Management System (RDBMS) was used for reliable storage of transaction information. This database was configured to handle thousands of concurrent on-line users.

- *Batch processing.* Several Java batch applications were created to process interface files and produce reports.

- *EDI.* Electronic Data Interchange was used to communicate between the *via* World Network system and the airline inventory systems (mainframes). A specialized, highly available server was used to perform the translation and communication.

- *Systems management and monitoring.* Interfaces were placed into the application to allow easy integration of monitoring tools. Interfaces between systems management tools and the Java applications had to be custom built, because no tools had Java interfaces at the time of construction.

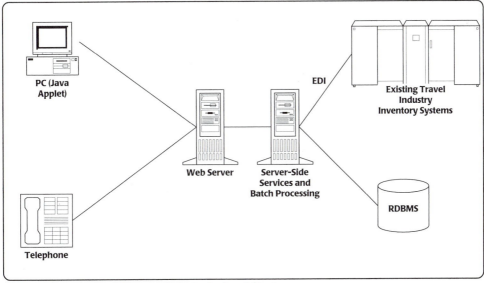

Figure 2.5 *via* World Network technical architecture

2.6 Pitfalls and Drawbacks of Using Java

Java was an emerging technology, and several of the challenges encountered were
results of the immaturity of the technology.

- *No on-line debugging tools for the Sun Solaris environment. via* World Network established UNIX as the application processing environment; however,
  powerful debugging tools emerged first for the Microsoft environment and
  only eventually were available in the Solaris environment.

- *The Java I/O on-line display libraries (Abstract Window Toolkit) had significant shortcomings.* Scroll list, tabbing, required fields, and resizeable window functionality had problems or lacked functionality for delivery of on-
  line business applications.

- *Knowledge of the Java technology for the use of business application development was just beginning to develop.* User communities generally were
  focused on the delivery of Internet-based applets downloaded from Web
  pages.

- *Skilled people and experts on Java technology were few and far between.* The team's skill base was built mostly from scratch, through real work and by attending conferences such as Java One.

- *Most companies had not used the Java technology for serious mission-critical systems.* The Java technology was early in its adoption and the prevailing business perception was that it had not been used for mission-critical business applications.

- *Development environments were not as integrated/developed as Visual Basic or PowerBuilder.* Java development environments did not have the GUI-based development tools nor were they well integrated with database access and construction. Products were beginning to emerge, but many of the tools developers had expected did not exist. Some tools are now beginning to emerge, and sites such as Gamelan (www.gamelan.com) on the Web are providing a richer base of products and source file examples. At the end of 1995, more than 500 Java resources were indexed on this site. By the end of 1996, more than 4,000 resources had been cataloged, with everything from education and network programming to application development tools.

- *There were few large projects from which to obtain comparable development effort metrics and input.* Because there were few similar large-scale Java technology implementations, it was difficult to predict the delivery effort or potential pitfalls.

2.7　Hindsight Is 20/20

While it is impossible to predict challenges and pitfalls that alternative approaches might have encountered, the following knowledge would have made the *via* World Network implementation easier.

2.7.1　Complexity of C-to-Java Interface

C libraries were used to access a RDBMS. A C interface had to be used, because the vendor had not yet developed a pure Java implementation and the standard for Java access to RDBMS had not yet been developed. This particular Java-to-C interface turned out to be the single biggest technology challenge. A number of conflicts in the management of memory were encountered between Java and the C libraries.

In this case, the interface between C and Java was problematic because the C code assumed that it was being called from C code. The need for more time and more experience to debug this interface was not anticipated.

2.7.2 Development Platform

Traditionally, professional software developers have preferred Solaris- and UNIX-based development over a Microsoft platform. *via* World Network's preference was for UNIX-based application development based on building of systems over the last ten years and the development of a number of custom tools that worked only on the Solaris environment. However, in this case, Solaris-based development slowed the project down. The Microsoft environment had on-line debugging tools, integrated development environments, runtime compilers, and testing tools months ahead of comparable tools for the Solaris environment. In hindsight, the *via* World Network team would have better spent the effort to convert their custom tools and focus the application developers toward a development environment with more tools.

2.7.3 Java's On-line Functionality

Although the Java technology is significantly better at network communications and image display than are traditional environment tools, Java 1.0 had significant shortcomings in the functionality of basic widgets (such as buttons and scroll lists), user control flow (tabbing and required fields, for example), and window management (for example, interwindow communication and window resizing). The effort required to plug the gaps in on-line functionality with either custom implementations or third-party software products was underestimated.

2.7.4 Technology Development Life Cycle

As a result of the dynamics and hype involved in an emerging technology, the project team was disappointed with delays in the delivery of Java-based technology. Java tools were slow in arriving, software providers' support of Java interfaces (relational database access, for example) was more marketing than reality, new releases of the Java Development Kit were delayed, and performance-enhancing tools (such as runtime compilers) were late and did not live up to initial expectations. The difficulties in the Java technology were not really problems so much as overly aggressive marketing plans for a new and emerging technology. Looking back on the original schedule, the project should have provided more buffer in the development schedule so that business application developers did not have to wait for the delivery of technology infrastructure.

2.8   Summary

The Java technology is ready for building mission-critical business systems. Large-scale, client/server, Internet-based applications can be built with the Java language. There are some pitfalls, because the technology is new and there is not a strong user base to draw on for experience and support. Based on the *via* World Network example, key considerations are as follows.

- Real-world, mission-critical business systems of over 15,000 function points can be built with the Java language.

- The Java language delivers productivity and application quality benefits in addition to the more well-known advantages of dynamic download and cross-platform support.

- The Java language can be used for more than just on-line applications, including server-based applications.

- Using Java technology as a platform is not without risks. With proper planning, these risks can be managed, resulting in a successful application development project.

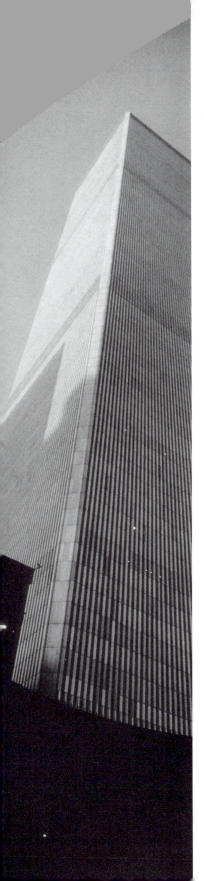

CHAPTER THREE

Case Study: Customer Sales Support

3.1 Introduction

This case study focuses on a business system used for call-center-based customer sales support. This particular case involves the conversion of an existing client/server system built in an integrated development environment (for example, PowerBuilder) to one that was built entirely using the Java language. The decision to perform a prototype conversion of the system was based on customer demand for a Java-based sales support solution.

3.2 Supporting Customer Sales

Catalog-based merchants generate a majority of their revenue through sales over the telephone rather than through a storefront. Rather than ship items around the nation and place them in warehouses and stores, catalog companies rely on their catalogs and call centers for customer sales. These call centers are generally available to customers and their requests 24 hours a day.

In many cases, these companies generate 80 to 90 percent of their yearly business during the two months prior to Christmas day. This presents challenges to the catalog companies, because they must stay in business 12 months of the year, but for the last two months they must multiply their call center capacity to support the increased volume of customers. This is especially challenging in light of the fact that customer service is critical to success. With the revenue stream generated through customer phone calls, corporate success depends on reliable, high-performance, high-quality, and efficient servicing of these phone calls. During the peak selling period, it is vital that a high level of customer service be maintained.

For these companies, costs and efficiencies are driven by the operation of call centers. Companies spend millions of dollars each year trying to increase the quality of their customer service while simultaneously lowering costs in call centers. For a large call center with more than 1,000 employees, reductions in the average call length of only a few seconds translate into significant cost reductions and more revenue as more customers are serviced.

In addition to operational efficiency goals, sales support call centers are often asked to leverage each customer call into a relationship-building opportunity. Each customer interaction represents an opportunity to learn more about customer demographics as well as to make additional, complementary sales. To support these activities, customer sales support organizations are supported by business systems that promote complementary sales. Understanding the customer requires analyses of both general customer trends and the individual buying patterns of specific customers. With this information, customer sales support clerks have an opportunity to increase the sales to each customer, thereby improving the efficiency of the call center operation.

3.3　Customer Sales Support Business Systems

As the business systems supporting customer sales call centers have developed, companies have typically relied on large mainframe systems to house critical customer information and perform the business support functions. These computers house and maintain repositories of customer and merchandise information. These repositories generally grow to significant size as the company tries to retain information about every customer it has serviced, allowing the company to target likely customers as well as gather demographic data. Even the information about a company's inventory can grow quite large as these companies typically have diversified the items they sell to encompass tens of thousands of items. Each item may have dozens of variations in sizes, color, and shape. Retaining inventory information, along with information about millions of customers, creates a repository that, in the past, required a large-scale mainframe for the appropriate reliability and processing speed.

Call center support personnel access this information and business functionality through dumb terminals or, more recently, personal computers that are directly connected to a mainframe. The applications the support personnel use provide simple retrieval functions and the ability to update customer information and generate orders. The configuration of a typical call center business system is shown in Figure 3.1.

For the call center to be successful, the business system must support the following characteristics.

- *Performance.* Performance is critical to the company's success. Slow response time directly results in decreased customer service, less revenue (through fewer calls processed), and higher costs per call. Ideally, each user request for information must complete in less than a second.

- *Repository size.* For a large call center with thousands of customers, a tremendous amount of data can be collected and analyzed (up to multiple terabytes). Using this data in support of sales activities requires the information to be accessed in a fast and reliable manner.

- *Reliability.* Overall system reliability is, perhaps, the most important aspect of the system. Downtime directly translates into lost revenue through lost calls and may translate into lost customers. Customer sales support systems require approximately 99.9% uptime.

- *Scalability.* As the company's sales volume fluctuates, the business system must be able to scale quickly by adding hundreds or even thousands of new

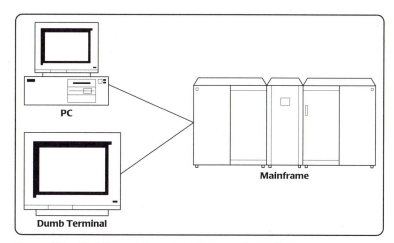

Figure 3.1   Mainframe-based system configuration

call center clerks. This scale must be achieved without jeopardizing reliability or performance of the business system.

As business volume grows and competition increases, heavier and heavier demands are placed on the business system. If the business system cannot scale, be reliable, provide appropriate performance, and access voluminous information, the company may not be able to grow and thrive in a competitive market.

3.4   A Client/Server Sales Support System

This case is based on an existing client/server sales support system that extended the model of call center business systems to client/server technology. This existing application was built with a client/server development tool (PowerBuilder) and provided powerful sales support functionality to the desktops of sales support personnel. This application leveraged a client/server relational database and existing legacy systems for access to certain information and business systems. This new client/server system had the following advantages over legacy, mainframe-based call center support systems.

- *Cost.* Client/server systems are less expensive to purchase and administer than mainframe-based systems.

- *Scalability.* It is much easier to scale a client/server system, by adding single, small increments, than to scale a mainframe system. This allows the call center to adapt more quickly to changing volumes.

- *Functionality.* The new client/server application retrieved client and merchandise information in multiple ways as opposed to just a key word or identity number. This functionality allowed customer sales support agents to respond flexibly to each customer call situation. The new application also allowed sales agents to view images of merchandise or even pictures of pages from a catalog. Sales agents used the image functionality to understand customer orders better and record them more accurately. The added functionality translated into opportunities for improved customer service and increased sales.

- *System performance.* A client/server system allows a call center to address performance issues more easily. A client/server system provides more processing power at the desktop and supports cost-effective, incremental

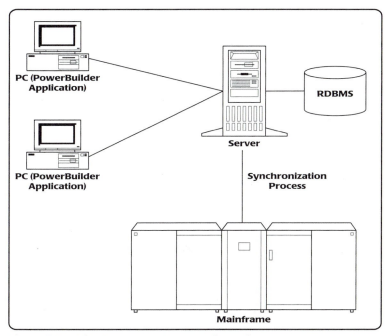

Figure 3.2   Client/server system configuration

growth on the server side. This growth can be achieved while maintaining standards of reliability and performance.

This client/server system has the system configuration shown in Figure 3.2.

3.5   Converting to the Java Language

The advantages of the existing client/server system were numerous and had been demonstrated in a number of customer sales support call centers. In early 1997, this client/server system was challenged by its customers to support additional capabilities, including low-cost network computers, Web access, support for a variety of customer desktops, support for new nontraditional user interfaces, and dynamic download of applications to a desktop. In response to customer demand, an investment decision was made to convert a significant portion of the existing application to the Java language. While this investment did not convert the entire client/server application, it did demonstrate enough of the application to prove basic call center support functionality and capability.

When developing the new Java application, the team did not start from scratch and redesign the existing client/server application. Instead, the team performed a conversion to the Java language. The intent was to keep both the GUI windows and functionality identical to those of the client/server application and thus save on development costs. Table 3.1 summarizes the time savings realized by converting from the existing PowerBuilder application rather than writing the system from scratch.

Table 3.1   Conversion metrics

Time to build original module:	X	
Time to test original module:	Y	
Time to convert module to Java:	4/10	X
Time to test converted module:	3/4	Y

To perform the conversion, the team created a standardized, step-by-step process for converting from PowerBuilder to the Java language. After several hundred days of conversion, the core functionality had been converted. The functionality had remained unchanged and there were only minor aesthetic differences between the two versions.

Even though on the surface the two applications appeared identical, the underlying structure of the system had changed. Rather than a two-tier architecture (GUI to database), the system had changed to a three-tier architecture (GUI to network service to database). This change was made to capture core processing logic and move it to server-based processing. Server-based processing enabled the new application to rapidly adopt and integrate new user interfaces (for example, telephone and personal digital assistant) without having to redevelop this core functionality for each new user interface.

3.6   Technology Solution

The technical implementation details of the system (see Figure 3.3) are summarized as follows.

- *A browser-based Java applet.* On the client side, a Java applet was created that incorporated images and had the "look and feel" of the original application.

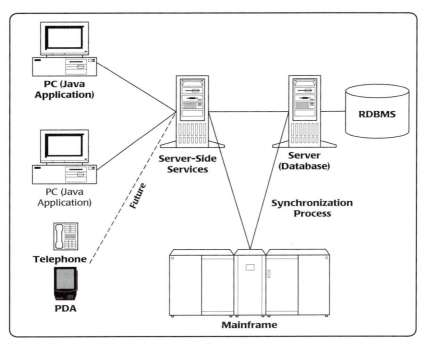

Figure 3.3   Java-based solution configuration

- *The server-side services executed within a multithreaded, continuously running process that received requests over the network, spawned the appropriate business process, and then returned the results.* Each service completed a simple business process, such as retrieving inventory data or updating an order.

- *Mainframe access was provided to the server-side services.* This allowed the application to retrieve and update master inventory information.

- *Database technology was deployed to ensure both high availability and successful handling of up to a terabyte of data.* To access the data, a Java-to-C interface was created, because commercial Java Database Classes (JDBC) implementations were not yet available.

3.7   Summary

The conversion of the core functionality of this client/server call center support application was completed on time, within budget, and was successfully demonstrated to call center users. This conversion demonstrated the following lessons regarding the Java technology and its ability to support business systems.

- Conversion from PowerBuilder to the Java language is possible within a reasonable amount of time and without sacrificing functionality.

- Java technology can support the demanding requirements of on-line call center applications.

- Java technology provides a robust environment for building three-tier client/server applications. In this case, the Java technology supported the migration of a two-tier application to one with an application server as the third tier.

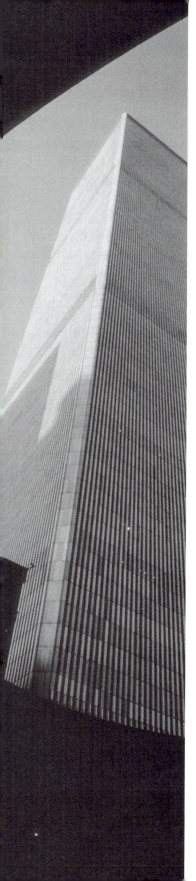

CHAPTER FOUR

Case Study: Customer Service Support

4.1 Introduction

This case study examines the use of Java technology in delivering a call center's customer support function. Specifically, this case reviews the use of the Java technology as an alternative vehicle for displaying customer bill information to call center support personnel. The existing customer service system provided bill display functionality but was not providing the performance or functionality necessary to support the growing requirements of the call center support personnel.

4.2 Supporting Customer Service Call Centers

Basic to many companies is the process of generating and mailing monthly customer bills. For companies that sell to the consumer market, large numbers of bills are generated every month. To support customer concerns regarding billing, companies provide call centers to answer questions and resolve issues. These call centers need access to billing information in order to serve customers adequately. The most effective manner in which to serve customers is for the support personnel to have access to a copy of the same bill that the customer sees. The sheer volume of bills large companies generate makes it impractical for a call center support person to locate and review an actual hard copy of a bill. The alternative is to display an on-line image of the customer's bill to the support personnel.

The on-line image allows the customer support personnel to answer questions about the bill both accurately and in a timely fashion. Through on-line viewing of a bill image, customer support personnel are able to improve customer service through fast, efficient, and accurate bill reconciliation. Critical to providing these benefits is adequate system performance. If the retrieval/display of bill images becomes a slow process, customer service is affected and costs increase, because each customer service call takes longer to resolve.

This case examines a company's existing bill image display system and the way in which the Java technology was used to provide a faster, more efficient, and more functional alternative.

4.3 Existing Business System

The customer support call center personnel were supported by a complex application developed in C++ and run on a NextPC. This application supported a variety of customer support functions including the bill image display capability. The existing bill image display system was failing to meet the customer sales support personnel's requirements in the following areas.

- *Speed.* The application was slow in retrieving images, which increased the time spent on-line with the customer.

- *Image display.* The image display application was built as a custom tool and was not easily adapted to emerging Internet technologies (for example, browsers, Web, and Java). Moreover, the display of bills was limited to the resolution of the scanned images of the bills.

- *Functionality.* The existing application did not have sufficient search capability for locating appropriate documents. The application also did not support on-line printing, faxing, and e-mailing of the bill.

- *Platform dependence.* The bill display application would run only on a single operating system. The call center needed bill image display capability on a number of operating system platforms.

- *Complexity and expense of platform.* To support the existing image display capability, a complex and expensive desktop computer was required.

4.4 Java-Based Solution

To address the shortcomings of the existing system, a Java-based approach was proposed. This approach addressed the challenges and issues regarding the current system and also provided additional functionality. The goals and objectives of the Java-based solution were as follows.

- *A large repository.* The call center required seven years of bill images to be available on-line. This information could be stored as approximately 1 terabyte of disk (on-line) storage and 5 terabytes of tape (off-line) storage.

- *Rapid access.* Despite the number and size of bill images, retrieval time had to be in the one-to-two-second range.

- *Accuracy.* The on-line image had to look identical to the customer's actual bill to allow the customer service agent to walk through the bill with the customer. Also, the agent needed the ability to zoom in on a section of the bill.

- *Integration.* The new display tool needed to be integrated with the existing system and not require additional log-ins or require the user to run any new application.

- *Functionality.* The new application had to allow the support agents to access key words in the bill image quickly and to support printing, faxing, and e-mailing of the bill image.

- *Platform support.* The display tool was required to work on a variety of desktops, not only ensuring widespread use but also eliminating costly desktop upgrades.

- *Adaptability.* The existing application took a long time to roll out, and new versions were installed slowly. The new application needed to be nimble and to respond more rapidly to new functionality/features requested by users.

The overall solution that was developed leveraged a Web browser, a Java applet, a third-party browser add-on, Java-based server-side services, and Java-based batch programs. The display functionality was developed as a combination of the browser, the Java applet, and a third-party product that ran within the browser. Combining these three components resulted in a robust, functional, and responsive solution that met the customer support center requirements.

Figure 4.1 is a graphical representation of the system's components. This solution demonstrated Java's ability to fill a variety of roles in a business system.

- *Applet.* The Java applet was dynamically downloaded within a browser and prompted the user for the criteria necessary to retrieve a bill image. In addition, this applet provided the ability to fax or e-mail the image.

- *Server-side services.* Within a Java-based server, client image display as well as fax and e-mail requests were received. The Java services within this server processed the requests and returned the appropriate error or success information.

- *Batch processing.* The bill images were created from the same file as the one used to create the printed bills. This file came from a mainframe and contained all of the printer commands necessary to generate a hard-copy bill. A batch application took the print output file and created a file of bill images and indices used to access those images. Another batch application loaded the indices and images into an RDBMS for retrieval by customer support agents.

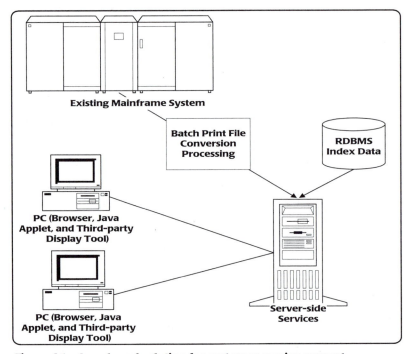

Figure 4.1   Java-based solution for customer service support

4.5 Technology Solution

The technical implementation details of the system are summarized as follows.

- *Applet.* A browser-based applet performed the basic on-line functions such as prompting the user for a password and collecting information for bill retrieval. Java code within the applet communicated to server-side services and requested image files.

- *Plug-in.* A third-party plug-in displayed an image and allowed the user to scroll and search within the image.

- *Images.* A large collection of image files was stored on a standard UNIX file system.

- *Batch applications.* Batch applications accepted a print file of images and converted the images to the necessary format for the browser plug-in.

- *Server-side services.* Server-side services performed simple functions, such as retrieval of the locations of the image files.

- *Database.* Configuration information was stored within a database. The database was accessed using a proprietary JDBC implementation.

- *Mainframe.* Files containing bill printing information were downloaded to a UNIX file system for processing.

4.6 Summary

The Java-based customer service support solution demonstrated the ability of the Java technology to meet the demanding needs of a call center's image display function. This solution demonstrated the following capabilities regarding the Java technology and its ability to support business systems.

- The integration of a Java applet, a Web browser, and a third-party browser add-on (or plug-in) was simple and effective. The interactions among the products was simple to implement, because no major technical obstacles were encountered.

- The combination of a Java applet, a Web browser, and a third-party browser add-on is a powerful tool in developing business systems. The browser provided a network-ready platform, the third-party product provided complex technology capability (image display and manipulation), and Java provided the "glue" necessary to build a solution customized to the customer support call center's requirements.

- The solution was platform independent and did not require complex and expensive hardware/operating systems.

- This solution demonstrated the rapid development capability of Internet technology (Java technology, browsers, and browser add-ons). The solution was developed starting from initial requirements gathering to user demonstration by five people in six weeks.

- Dynamic download capabilities of the Java technology supported rapid upgrades to the bill display solution. The call center environment contained thousands of users in multiple locations. Dynamic download capability is a dramatic improvement in the speed with which applications can be adapted to meet user needs.

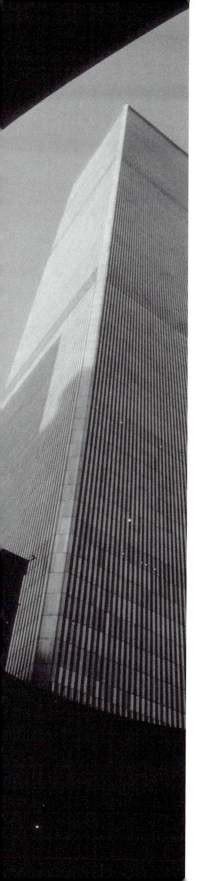

CHAPTER FIVE

Case Study: Human Resource Service Delivery

5.1 Introduction

This case study examines the use of the Java technology in delivering human resource data and functionality to corporate employees. The Java technology was used as a tool for enabling an innovative approach to improving the efficiency and service delivery of human resource services to employees. Human resource functions today are performed through a combination of manual processing, software products, and outsourced service providers. Simplifying the process, lowering cost, and improving the service delivery of human resource functions were the objectives of the solution documented in this case.

5.2 Delivering Human Resource Services

All large corporations make use of human resource functions to manage the growth and development of personnel. Human resource functions vary from company to company, but generally include such activities as payroll and salary administration, recruiting, and career development.

The delivery of human resource functions has historically been manually intensive with teams of people being dedicated to servicing the administration of personnel resources. Over time, software products that automate a variety of human resource administration and tracking functions have emerged. In addition, companies have begun to outsource not only the automation but also the operation of human resource functions. Payroll processing and benefit administration (for example, health and 401K programs) are human resource functions that many companies outsource to service providers.

The use of software products and service providers help companies improve service delivery and reduce the costs of human resource functions. Unfortunately, the combination of software technology installations and the outsourcing of functions complicates delivery of human resource services. Employees are often required to store personnel data in multiple systems and learn different processes and user interfaces for each human resource function. In addition, there is no consolidated source of employee human resource information for employers to use in understanding the human resource needs of their employees. Likewise, the lack of consolidated information makes it difficult for service providers to improve service delivery and reduce costs beyond their current software technology or outsourced service.

5.3   Solution Prototype

This case study tracks Java's role in a prototype developed to address the inefficiencies and costs in the current environment of human resource service delivery. The prototype's purpose was to demonstrate the ability to create a single, trusted location for the storage and maintenance of human resource information and to personalize the information, allowing employees to manage their own personnel data easily. This single location would be used by employees to maintain their human resource profiles, by employers to manage a coordinated human resource function, and by service providers to identify opportunities to improve service delivery and decrease costs.

The functions envisioned in the overall, full-scale solution included:

- *Payroll.* Allow employees to view paycheck information on-line.

- *Employee information.* Allow employees to view and change personnel data such as address and family details.

- *Benefits.* Allow employees to view and change benefit options such as dental and medical plans.

- *Retirement plan (401K).* Allow employees to view their elections and current balances in 401K funds.

- *Corporate information.* Allow employees to view company policies, information regarding company events, and company financial reports.

- *News.* Provide employees access to a current news source.

- *Travel.* Provide employees with the ability to plan and book travel.

- *Other.* The system was intended to be flexible to allow for the addition of other functions as necessary. It also allowed the user to create a "personalized" space by customizing the user interface and storing personnel information.

This single, trusted, and consolidated source for human resource information and functionality was designed to deliver the following benefits.

- *Easy access to information.* Employees could access their personnel information, benefit information, and corporate information from their desks or from their homes. No longer were employees forced to contact a human resource representative during normal business hours.

- *Current information.* By not printing benefit information, company policies, and personnel information, it became easier to keep this information up to date, because only a single electronic copy was maintained.

- *Reduced cost.* By virtualizing many of the human resource functions, costs were reduced in the areas of hard-copy information distribution and collection and human resource labor.

- *Adaptability to new user interfaces.* The system supported the concept of network-based services that were not tied to a single user interface. This approach supported the rapid adoption of new user interfaces such as voice recognition and personal digital assistants.

- *Single location of employee data.* Rather than spread human resource functions across multiple heterogeneous systems, everything could be combined into a single system. This single location approach would simplifiy access and maintenance of important employee data.

- *Connecting service providers to employees.* A new low-cost distribution channel from service providers to customers was created. Service providers could leverage this channel to make new and expanded offers (such as 401K, health benefits, etc.) to their corporate customers.

The development team was a small group of highly skilled software developers. They quickly learned the Java language and began developing a full-featured prototype. After only a few months of development, the team created an end-to-end prototype with a highly interactive on-line application and server-side services to support the functionality. Owing to the Java advantages of Internet computing capabilities and increased developer productivity, the project team was able to complete the work well within schedule and budget according to the original requirements.

5.4   Technology Solution

Through the use of Internet and intranet technologies, this system would reduce the actual cost of human resource functions and significantly increase the level of service from an employee's point of view. Figure 5.1 is an overview of the major technology components of this system.

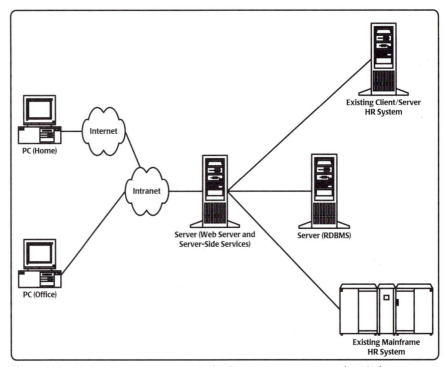

Figure 5.1   Technology components for human resource service delivery

The prototype system has the following technology components.

• *JavaScript user interface.* The GUI application was created primarily with JavaScript. HTML and Java were included as necessary to supplement Java-Script.

• *Both Internet and intranet access.* A key objective of the prototype system was to allow employees secure access to human resource information either from home or from the office through Internet and intranet technologies.

• **Web server and third-party JavaScript interface.** A third-party product was used to communicate with the JavaScript GUI. These functions within the Web server sent and received messages between the client and the server-side services.

• *Server-side services.* These services are Java functions that service requests by the client. These services perform business activities to carry out the human resource functions and to communicate with the rest of the solution (including a database for employee information as well as existing human resource systems).

• *Database.* The system used an RDBMS as the primary location for storage and retrieval of employee and company information.

• *Batch applications.* The Java language was used to create batch applications to generate reports and process interface files.

• *Interfaces to existing and other human resource systems.* The system was initially built to interface with a single human resource system with the intention of interfacing to other human resource systems in the future.

5.5 Summary

The prototype development of this human resource service delivery system involved a variety of technologies, platforms, and software products. This case study demonstrated the following.

• Server-side systems based on the Java technology can be deployed and integrated with existing business systems and software products.

- The Java language can be used for delivering server-side applications that communicate to users through a browser interface over both the Internet and internal corporate intranets.

- The Java technology can be successfully leveraged with other software technologies (for example, Web servers and Web browsers) to deliver business solutions.

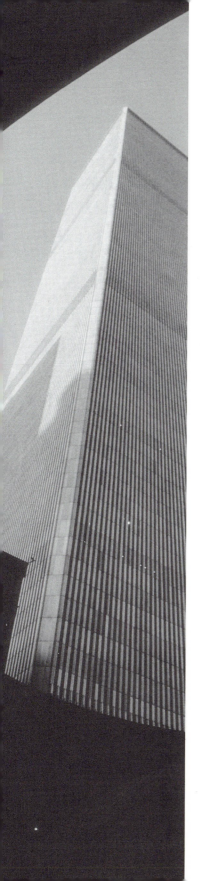

CHAPTER SIX

An Enabling Technology

6.1 New Opportunities

Every so often, new technologies create new opportunities for companies to achieve competitive advantage through improved products, lowered operating costs, or better customer service. The advent of client/server technology allowed companies to distribute computing power to individual business departments, creating more efficient ways to operate the business and meet customer service requirements. The emergence of GUIs allowed simpler, more intuitive access to business applications, promoted productivity gains, and lowered the costs of user training. The emergence of the Internet provided businesses with the opportunity to leverage a low-cost channel to reach millions of customers around the world. In each of these cases, the opportunities created by the new technology affected how businesses operated and went to market.

Whenever a new technology has the potential to improve how a business operates or markets its products, visionary companies seize the opportunities of the technology, and leverage its potential. Other companies take a wait-and-see attitude about whether the technology either fulfills its potential or fails to meet expectations. It is at this point that companies begin understanding and applying the power of the new technology to create new ways of doing business. If the technology proves itself viable and the business advantage is clearly understood, the technology becomes mainstream and many companies begin to deploy it.

In 1998, Java technology began to reach the status of a mainstream solution. Enough companies have worked with Java to prove its capability to provide new business benefits. When developing Java applications, a company is able to leverage opportunities such as:

- *Multiple deployment options.* Applications can be either dynamically downloaded or locally installed on customer or user desktops.

- *Network computers.* These low-cost computers are well suited for clerical activities and can have a significant impact on reducing maintenance expenses when compared with traditional PCs.

- *Best price/performance platform.* Platform independence gives companies more choices in deploying the business system and avoids platform lock-in.

- *Integrating Internet technologies.* Java technology is the glue that ties together Internet technologies in providing a complete solution for business application delivery.

6.2　Multiple Deployment Options

Prior to the advent of the Internet, companies distributed software products on floppy disks through commercial software chains. Since the emergence of the Internet, companies have been able to distribute their software products electronically. Customers are able to download software from a company's Web site, making it significantly easier to release new versions of software.

An option for companies in eliminating the physical distribution of software is implementation of applications through the Web by using HTML pages. These pages can, in many cases, implement the functionality that once required software to be loaded onto a PC. Unfortunately, for complex business applications, HTML may not provide the functionality, capability, or responsiveness necessary to meet user requirements. This is where Java comes in. Java supports the dynamic downloading of an application to a user's desktop at the point at which a Web page is accessed. This capability supplements HTML in that complex, responsive applications can be built in a low-cost and easy-to-use manner.

Even though dynamic download has been touted as a primary benefit of Java, Java programs do not necessarily need to be dynamically downloaded. Java supports local installation of applications on a user's computer much like installation of traditional desktop applications. Businesses are able to develop Java applications first and determine the nature of the deployment based on the responsiveness of the application and the needs of the user.

For example, in *via* World Network, the application used by travelers was installed locally on users' desktops. The intent of the decision to install locally was to ensure that heavy users of the application would not incur the overhead and delay of dynamic download of the application. As expected, this resulted in an application that had good response time but required users to go through a simple installation process.

To roll out this application more rapidly to users who did not require immediate application response, the application was converted from a locally installed application to a dynamically downloaded application. The conversion of the application took less than a week to prototype and prove. Within a month, the same application could be locally installed or dynamically downloaded from a Web server with no changes in the application logic. The month of work was spent in configuring the dynamically downloaded application in a manner that achieved the fastest possible download time.

The downside of local installation through Java is the loss of simple and rapid deployment of new versions of the application. With applets tied to a Web page, the user gets a new copy of the application each time the Web page is accessed. With applets, new releases of software need only be installed on the Web server where the Web page is located. By loading a Java application on to a PC, the challenge of upgrading the Java application is the same as for any traditional desktop application. Listed below are two ways in which the impact of upgrades for locally installed applications can be minimized.

- *Third-party products.* Companies such as Marimba have begun to focus on ways in which Java applications can be installed on a user's desktop and updated as needed. While these products do not take advantage of Java's dynamic download capability, they provide an infrastructure for rolling out new versions of applications with minimal effect on users.

- *Pull versus push metaphor.* In the past, business applications were "pushed" to users. New versions of applications were sent to users, requiring a significant investment on the part of the corporation to send and coordinate a new version installation. The Internet has developed and proved the concept of "pull" application updates. By using Web browsers and Web servers, applications can be "pulled" down by users in much the same way Internet browsers are updated by millions of users each year.

6.3 Network Computers

Network computers have been widely described as a powerful approach to lowering the costs associated with managing and deploying desktop client systems. Network computers load their operating systems and applications through the network and do not require local hard drive support. Network computer advantages include lower implementation and system support costs. It has been estimated that network computers could save thousands of dollars per user per year in comparison with the support and maintenance costs of traditional PC desktops. Network computers are best suited for clients who use the same applications throughout the day (for example, call centers and clerical support).

Java technology is well suited for network computing applications. Most network computers are designed to provide support for Java capability; therefore, Java can accurately be described as a development language for network computers.

There is little debate about network computers being less expensive to implement, operate, and maintain than traditional PC desktops. What is in doubt is the viability of network computers in solving real-world business problems. The challenge for network computers is the lack of existing solutions and software. Network computers emerged at the same time as Java and lacked a significant installed base of business application software to run on this platform. Because of the immaturity of the software base, it is unlikely that during the late 1990s network computers will replace a significant number of existing client/server systems. What is more likely is that network computers will be used for new applications focused on clerical or support functions that have either no computer or only dumb terminal support. In these situations, network computers can leverage their low cost of implementation and support to facilitate the development of Java business systems.

6.4 Best Price/Performance

Java technology's platform independence allows companies to focus more attention on developing business systems than on technology. In most complex business system development efforts, significant time and energy are spent in choosing the optimum platform for delivering the application. This decision typically has to be made early in the development life cycle because of the impact a platform has on the way in which an application is developed. In addition, benchmarking and performance estimates are generally performed only on a single platform as a result of challenges in supporting the development of applications that will run on multiple platforms.

Java technology's platform independence provides a powerful new capability for choosing the right platform for meeting business needs. Java technology lets companies defer the final choice of the production platform until after the application has been built and the company understands the true requirements of the system. The company is then in a better position to choose the best price/performance platform for its business application.

While this sounds too good to be true, a real-life example will help in driving home the point of this business advantage. The marketing of the *via* World Network application identified a significant competitive advantage by guaranteeing lowest fares to business travelers. The downside was that three times more processing power would be required for each request. The challenge was cost-effective delivery of the additional processing. Obtaining three times the processing power with the current platform was too expensive. The option chosen was to move the most intensive processing operations to a lower-cost computing platform. The cost of the new platform was one-tenth that of the old one. The technology that made it possible to use the alternative platform was Java. Building the entire business logic as a Java system allowed *via* World Network to move processing-intensive operations (with minimal effort) to a lower-cost platform.

Java technology was designed for the development of platform-independent applications, but developments in 1997 and 1998 created differences in Java implementations. (For example, both Microsoft and Hewlett Packard developed Java technology that was not compliant with the specification published by Sun Microsystems.) In order to take full advantage of platform independence, companies must continue to monitor the differences among Java implementations and understand the resulting impact on their applications.

6.5 Integrating Internet Technologies

The emergence of the Internet raised the awareness within the business community of complementary technologies. Web servers, communication protocols, Web browsers, security products, firewalls, HTML, and CGIs (Common Gateway Interfaces) are just a start. Creation of an effective, robust business solution for applications on the Web requires a combination of all these technologies into one seamless system.

Java provides a platform geared to leveraging of Web, Internet, and intranet computing technologies. Java technology is the glue that joins these technologies and provides a platform for building business applications through the following capabilities.

- *Internet protocol support.* Java technology supports communication to external applications through the use of the HyperText Transfer Protocol (HTTP). HTTP is the basic network protocol used for all Web communications and is also a standard format used for communicating through corporate firewalls. By supporting this Internet-friendly protocol, Java makes it simple to build business applications that communicate with each other over the Internet. For example, a client application might be downloaded by a user and need to communicate with another application through the Internet. By using HTTP for this communication, the application can be easily rolled out to users who are protected by corporate firewalls.

- *Simple intranet communications.* The Java language provides a simple and powerful set of functions for communicating with other network-based services within an intranet. An intranet is a corporate private network that uses the Internet network protocol: Transmission Control Protocol/Internet Protocol (TCP/IP).

- *Browser intercommunication.* Java technology supports a simple interface to browsers. The interface can be used to instruct the browser to load a Web page. This is a powerful technique by which a Java application can support context-sensitive help. For example, when the user requests help text, the Java application can "tell" the browser to load the page that contains the appropriate help information. In this way, Java applications can leverage the browser and avoid the need to reinvent this functionality. In each of the case studies outlined in Chapters 2 and 4, the Java-based business system leveraged the capability to communicate with the browser to deliver more functionality to the user.

By integrating all of these technologies, a Java application provides a way in which Internet, intranet, and Web technologies can be seamlessly brought together for users. Business applications are built faster by leveraging simple interfaces to these technologies rather than having to develop in-house, custom integrations.

There is a downside to the use of Internet and intranet technologies. The business must have a strong understanding of these related technologies if the overall system is to be cleanly implemented. A poorly designed network or improperly configured browser will result in a poor user experience even if the Java application is flawless.

6.6 Summary

Java offers new business opportunities for companies to improve their operations or create new ways to meet the needs of their customers. The key messages in how Java computing is a technology that enables new business opportunities are as follows.

- Through multiple deployment options, companies have more flexibility in meeting the needs of a varied user or customer community.

- The promise of low-cost network computers is enabled by Java's ability to bring business application functionality and capability to this platform.

- Through platform independence, Java gives the company the opportunity to reduce operational cost and improve service delivery by migrating the business application to the best price/performance platform.

- Through Java technology's simple integration with Internet technologies, companies can easily and effectively develop rich and flexible intranet applications.

CHAPTER SEVEN

Is Java a Fad?

7.1 The DeLorean Effect

In the early days of Java, it was easy to see the advantages of building business systems based on Java. Java's platform independence, dynamic download capabilities, and integration with the Internet were powerful and compelling advantages. The primary disadvantage of Java, at least in its early stages, was not security, stability, or even performance. Of these well-publicized issues, experience in 1996 showed that security issues were overplayed. Java had proven to be stable, and performance issues could be addressed through smart application design. The key concern revolved around Java's ability to generate widespread enthusiasm in both consumers and third-party product suppliers. Without broad adoption and consumer demand, a rich technology environment with a strong base of functionality and vendor alternatives would not emerge. Java might have become the "DeLorean" of the computer industry: a beautiful and elegant technology, but with a small customer base, no parts suppliers, and no local garage that would touch it.

7.2 The Legacy of Fad Technologies

Early Java applications had to build a number of custom utilities commonly found in other programming languages, including message communication, help facilities, and client/server communications. Java technology was new and powerful, but robust, proven solutions were few. Technology pioneers often are able to build the custom components necessary for the first one to two years. The danger, however, is in having to support these custom components forever. If a technology market does not develop, these custom solutions are not, over time, replaceable with supported vendor solutions. This leads to a long-term challenge in that the custom components are critical to the system's operation but are not supported by any vendor. Worse, the creators of the custom components have usually moved on to other pioneering technologies. Invariably, the technology becomes antiquated. Over time, the system grows weaker and weaker as it is patched with a variety of custom improvements that are not part of a long-term product strategy. Eventually, one of, or a combination of, the following three scenarios occurs.

- The business system is frozen as changes in the technology cannot be reliably implemented without affecting system availability.

- Support costs are artificially high, motivating personnel with key skills to continue supporting an old and antiquated technology.

- The system undergoes an expensive and time-consuming overhaul or port to a new technology.

These scenarios are, unfortunately, all too common in the world of information technology. Examples of failed technology include software languages (such as Smalltalk, 4GLs, and LISP), shifts in operating system technology, and changes in GUI technology and in the use of artificial intelligence packages. In all of these cases, many custom utilities that were intended to be short-term solutions turned into long-term support challenges.

7.3 Java's Popularity Encourages New Resources

The primary source of information regarding a new technology is the original vendor. The support and information are generally thin, and the challenges faced by the application developer are new to the vendor as well. In some rare cases, other users of the technology are found and some useful information is exchanged. More often than not, however, the key challenges must be faced, and either overcome or circumvented, by each early adopter.

Even before the 1.0 release of Java technology, it was clear that Java was different. The vendor, Sun Microsystems, was stretched, because the interest level was so great that its JavaSoft division was overwhelmed by customer requests. Although this posed problems in resolving detailed technology and strategy questions, the benefits were tremendous. This interest generated a rapid growth in new and powerful third-party support resources.

Early Java development (1996) was aided by two resources on the Web: Digital Expresso and Gamelan (www.gamelan.com). Digital Expresso was an emerging electronic magazine that summarized the key threads in the Java newsgroup, reviewed the major Java announcements in an editorial, provided links to new Java resources, and maintained a list of Java contacts. Digital Expresso's newsgroup summary played a big part in helping Java users identify issues early and make better-informed application development decisions. Digital Expresso also helped in finding early Java examples that expedited the implementation of prototypes.

Gamelan is a Web site that bills itself as "the premier Java resource site." Examples, links, and source code samples can be found in a wide variety of categories from education to multimedia to games to science. In early 1996, more than 600 resources were cataloged on Gamelan from countries as diverse as Japan, Australia, Germany, and Russia. More than anything else, Gamelan gave early Java users confidence that a technology market was emerging that would grow into a significant resource over time.

The year after its first production release, Java technology's popularity grew quickly. There were early signs of this growth, such as Java technology's being mentioned in business magazines including *Business Week*, but the first real indication that Java was different occurred in May 1996 at the Java One conference. The conference was sold out and developers from around the world were not only passionate in their praise but also demanding of Sun and other vendors in forcing the rapid adoption and improvement of Java-based tools. The global growth of Java computing was evidenced at the conference but also by the continued worldwide contributions to Gamelan and to the ever-growing number of Java articles, magazines, and books. Another gauge is the number of book titles found on the shelves of major booksellers. In early 1996, less than ten books about Java had been published. On a trip to the same bookstore in early 1997, one would have found more than 100 Java titles.

7.4 Developer Acceptance of Java

Java has reached a broader community of developers than those who traditionally used only market-leading products (Microsoft's Visual Basic and Sybase's PowerBuilder, for example). How then has Java's acceptance exceeded that of market-leading application development products? Java has distinguished itself from the traditional development environment to reach a wider, more diverse audience in the following key ways.

- *The number of downloads of the Java Development Kit (JDK).* Although Sun's JDK is not for sale, it can be downloaded without cost. In March of 1998, Sun Microsystem's James Gosling stated that 2.5 million downloads of the JDK had occurred since Java technology was first released. By being free, Java does not restrict access to only those who can pay for it. If only 10 percent of downloads result in significant use of Java technology and therefore are counted as "users," Java computing has a significant installed base.

- *Java computing is a global technology.* Because Java is free and accessible over the Internet, more than 40 million people (with access to the Internet in 1996) have access to Java technology. No sales force, support staff, import restrictions, or customs duties stand in the way of Java's use around the world.

- *The corporate community's interest in Java technology.* Java computing has built a strong interest in the business community, as evidenced by articles in *The Wall Street Journal* and *Business Week.* Java technology's capabilities and exposure to executive corporate management have far surpassed those of Visual Basic or PowerBuilder. In many ways, Java computing has ridden the recent upsurge in interest in the Internet. As they did with the Internet, corporations are excited and aggressively pursuing the potential of this technology to achieve competitive advantage and lower the costs of doing business. A Zona Research study released in mid-1997 concluded that 47 percent of the companies surveyed were currently using Java technology and that the remaining 53 percent expected to use Java within the next 12 months. This study was released only 18 months after Java technology's first production release.

- *Java technology reaches a wider spectrum of developers.* Scientific, technical, academic, business, and casual developers are interested in Java development. An example of this broad range of interest can be found on sites such as Gamelan, where currently there are more than 9,000 resources and examples of Java implementations are cataloged. This broad range of interest is attributable to several advantages that Java computing has over other development languages and tools.
  - Java is free of charge.
  - Its dynamic download capability can enliven Web pages.

- It is a full-featured, object-oriented language that combines the best technology features of C, C++, and languages such as Smalltalk.
- It is platform independent.

- *Browser support.* By running within browsers such as Netscape Navigator and Microsoft's Internet Explorer, Java technology instantly reaches 40 million Internet users. Java's capabilities are constantly demonstrated to users around the world. Users have become familiar with Java computing and have begun to think of it as the language of the Internet, and this becomes a self-fulfilling cycle when a user sees an interesting Java application and decides to implement something similar. Exposure to a wide audience leads to greater use in the developer community.

7.5 Third-Party Product Support for Java Computing

The test of a technology's staying power is in the maturation and relevance of third-party product support. Have products supporting Java applications emerged and reduced the need for custom development? Do these products serve the broad market of business systems, or are they solutions for only a narrow range of challenges? The following are examples of scenarios in which third-party product support for Java development reduced the amounts of custom development necessary in the case studies described in Chapters 2 through 5.

- *Application server.* In early 1996, source code for a sample Java application server was used to demonstrate the feasibility of Java server-side applications. While the server did not meet the technology needs of the application and the code was not used, this example application server code demonstrated the power of Java technology as a platform for building application servers.

- *GUI widgets.* An application needed to display a tabbed folder background as part of its design. A source code implementation of tabbed folders was found and purchased through the Internet, saving significant time and expense.

- *On-line development.* A number of competing tools for painting and generating Java applications are available, resulting in competition in price and functionality. Java development projects have the opportunity to analyze multiple tools and choose the one that has the best function/feature and price point to meet the business system's needs.

- *Java-capable browser as a desktop.* By executing applications through a browser, the browser's secure communication facilities and network configuration tools are leveraged. Internet network communications often must be secure; use of the security protocols that exist in browsers simplifies the implementation effort. The use of browsers also saves significant development time through their support of the setup and maintenance of network configuration settings.

- *Browser plug-ins.* In building a document management system, images of customer bills were to be displayed to customer service agents. The bill images had to be searchable, had to support a zoom capability, and had to be easily printed on the network. Through the combination of a browser plug-in and a Java applet, a powerful solution was obtained. The Java application captured the user's search criteria, and the browser plug-in rapidly and successfully displayed and manipulated the bill image.

- *Java class file enhancements.* Custom Java utilities built by one project team were replaced by a third-party product to achieve performance improvements. The custom infrastructure implemented extensions to the Java language in the areas of variable manipulation (dates, strings, arrays, etc.). While the functionality of the custom utilities met the business requirements, the vendor product also met the requirements and was more than 50 percent faster in execution.

7.6   The Pace of Acceptance

Java technology's adoption rate continues to accelerate, which will lead to a healthy, profitable, and mature market for third-party product solutions. Signs of Java technology's increasing acceptance include:

- **JDK downloads.** The JDK continues to be downloaded by users and developers from around the world.

- *The use of the Internet and Java-capable browsers continues to grow.* As Internet use becomes common, more and more users will be exposed to the capabilities of Java technology, leading to increased use as a solution to business challenges.

- *Number of solutions on Gamelan.* The Gamelan Java catalog continues to grow in size and richness. The Gamelan site grew from 500 Java references (early 1995) to more than 9,000 in little more than a year and a half.

- *Number of third-party Java product solutions.* Java computing's support through third-party products increased dramatically during 1996. From a basis of zero, JavaSoft published a provider catalog in October 1996 with references to thousands of Java products and solutions from providers around the world.

- *Java One conference.* The second Java One conference held in April 1997 in San Francisco was attended by thousands of developers from around the world. The conference sessions demonstrated real-world Java solutions in both the technical and business communities.

7.7 Summary

Long-term success of business applications depends on choosing a platform that not only meets technology requirements but also grows and adapts over time. Choose a technology platform poorly, and the business will be forced to struggle with ever-increasing support costs as well as jeopardize the business system's ability to meet customer needs over the long term. Third-party product support is the essential element that ensures that a technology will move beyond the fad stage. Java technology is well positioned to continue as a growing and thriving technology platform for building business applications for the following reasons.

- Adoption of Java technology has mirrored the rise in interest in the Internet.

- Software companies have incorporated Java products into their strategic plans.

- Java computing has been embraced by a wider community of users and developers than has any other development technology.

- Time-to-market reductions can be achieved by leveraging the experience and tools built from different parts of the Java community.

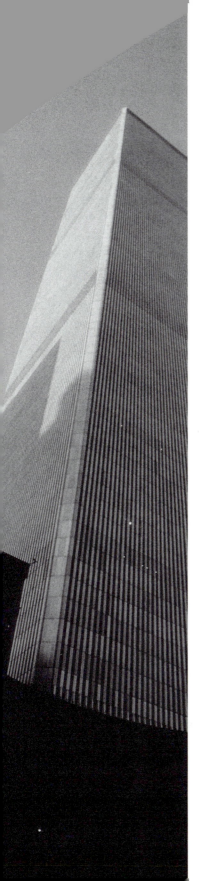

CHAPTER EIGHT

Converting Existing Business Systems

8.1   Upgrades to Business Systems

Decades of computer technology have changed the way companies do business. All Fortune 500 companies have significant investments in technology. Those companies that choose not to incorporate computers into their business fall by the wayside. Systems technology offers too many benefits in productivity and customer service enablement to be ignored by a modern business.

Even though companies must use computer technology to survive, this does not imply that technology guarantees success. If implemented incorrectly, building a new business system can be a financial disaster that yields no benefits. Even if implemented correctly, maintaining computer systems is costly. To compound matters, systems must be continuously upgraded to keep maintenance costs down and to keep up with the competition.

Upgrading a legacy business system to newer technology is usually an expensive endeavor. New technology generally does not integrate well with older technology, and existing systems usually require application rewrites to incorporate upgrades. Migrating to new technology is a fact of life for most companies, and therefore most are willing to struggle in order to perform a successful conversion.

One of the most difficult and time-consuming activities in upgrading a system is the recoding of applications. Legacy system upgrades usually involve rewriting older lines of code in a newer programming language. This upgrading eventually reduces maintenance costs and may offer competitive advantages as newer programming languages enable new business opportunities. Rewriting programs can, however, be tedious, and it may take more time to reprogram than it took to program the original system.

Java computing represents a new technology that can provide businesses with powerful new competitive capabilities and cost savings. These benefits are powerful inducements for companies to consider converting legacy systems to Java technology. However, even when converting a legacy system to Java technology, a company must consider the cost/benefits of performing this work.

8.2   How "Clean" Is the Legacy System?

Before deciding whether or not to convert an existing system to Java, it is important to understand the legacy system's current state. Existing applications fall over a spectrum of "cleanness." Some systems are well-written, follow strict coding standards, have common frameworks, contain easy-to-understand code, and are easy to maintain. On the other end of the spectrum are systems that are poorly written, inconsistent in style, complex in design, and virtually impossible to maintain. Most systems lie somewhere between the well-architected and poorly written.

The cost of converting a business system to Java is directly related to the quality or "cleanness" of the legacy system (see Figure 8.1). A system on the well-written end of the spectrum should be considered as a candidate for conversion. A company with a poorly written system should strongly consider rewriting the system rather than converting. A conversion will generally maintain the characteristics of the legacy system, while a rewrite will allow designers to improve the quality and cleanness of the overall system. In either case, the cost of converting or rewriting the system must be balanced against the business benefits of leveraging Java technology.

This chapter discusses the conversion of systems that are on the well-written side of the spectrum. It offers insights and lessons learned on how to perform the conversion process. Once the decision has been made to convert a well-written system, there are two points to consider. The first is how to automate the conversion process as much as possible. The second is the skill level of the programming

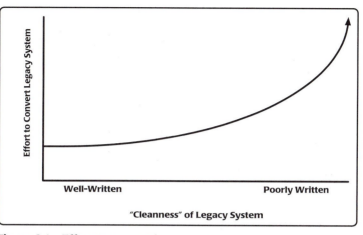

Figure 8.1   Effort to convert legacy system

team. If none of the legacy system developers are available and if the developers are not skilled programmers, a conversion may be difficult or even out of the question. It takes a talented, energetic team to convert a large business system successfully from one language to another.

8.2.1 Easing the Pain of Conversion

Fortunately, the Java programming language has a number of characteristics that help ease the pain of converting existing systems. The following points illustrate how to leverage Java technology in a conversion.

- *The Java language is similar to existing languages.* The Java programming language is based on existing programming languages. The best of C and C++ can be found in the Java language, and programmers familiar with these languages should find it easy to understand Java code. This fact makes the conversion from C or C++ less painful, because much of the programming syntax does not change.

- *Java programming can be object-oriented or procedural in nature.* Most older systems are written in a procedural fashion, and a few have been written with an object-oriented style. Java is flexible enough to support either object-oriented or procedural programming (or even both at the same time). Because the Java language is a simpler object programming language than C++, it can be used by either experienced or inexperienced C++ object developers, which further eases conversion concerns.

- *The Java language is a full-featured language.* C and C++ developers may be skeptical of converting to Java technology because they are accustomed to the flexibility of these languages; however, the Java language has all of the features required to build large business systems. The Java language is a full-featured programming language that actually offers more functionality than C or C++.

- *Continuing to leverage complex legacy C or C++ code.* If an existing system has complex C or C++ code that is considered difficult to convert, it may be appropriate to leave key sections of the legacy application in C or C++. Java technology supports access of C and C++ code from the Java application. The downside of this technique is the loss of platform portability and dynamic download capability; however, in certain cases the preservation of complex legacy code should be used to minimize the costs and risks of conversion.

8.3   A Structured Conversion Approach

When converting a "clean" legacy system to Java technology, a company should take a structured approach. The following approach breaks down the conversion into a step-by-step process. Although the specifics of this process are for conversions from C or C++, this process also generally supports conversions to Java technology from other languages. Following this or a similarly structured approach will save time, reduce cost, and yield a better business system.

8.3.1   Automating Simple, Repetitive Syntax Changes

In the Java language, there are many similarities in syntax to C or C++, but there are also minor differences. These minor differences are easily converted, and the business should take the time to write, find, or purchase a conversion tool. One place to research is the World Wide Web, where various solutions are available. Many developers have already addressed the problem of conversion, and some of these solutions are available at no cost.

8.3.2   Interfaces to Third-Party Products

Because Java technology is new, not all third-party products have been upgraded to or integrated with the Java platform. Even if the vendor has built a Java language version, it is likely that the legacy system will be on an older version of the product that does not support a Java interface. If a system requires a C or C++

interface, the business should use the Java native interface support to build a Java "wrapper" around the interface.

8.3.3 Preserving Complex Logic

If the legacy system contains sections of complex C or C++ code that would be difficult to convert, an option is to leave this logic in its original state. Through the Java native interface facility, a Java layer is placed around the legacy logic. This technique avoids some of the most challenging and risky steps in a conversion.

8.3.4 Reorganizing Source Files into Packages

Java uses "packages" to organize the source files of an application. Before the system is converted, the source files must be inventoried and it must be determined how best to organize the source files into Java packages. The conversion team will be required thoroughly to understand the Java concept of packages.

8.3.5 Leveraging Existing Development Tools and Processes

By maintaining as many existing tools and processes as possible, the development of a business application can be completed with less time and cost. Java application development requires some changes, but may not require a completely new set of tools and processes. Before preceding further with the conversion, the company should consider how best to leverage the existing environment during and after the conversion. Chapter 20 is an in-depth analysis of the impact of using Java technology on existing development tools and processes.

8.3.6 Converting C/C++ Constants into Variables within Java classes

Constants should be converted into Java variables using three qualifiers: "public," "static," and "final." When programming, developers define constants in their applications, but the technique for doing this in Java is quite different. The easiest way to provide constants is to define Java "classes" that contain variables using the public, static and final qualifiers.

8.3.7 Creating a Java Class for Each Source File

Rather than try to create a pure object-oriented design when converting C applications to the Java language, time can be saved by simply treating each existing source file as a single Java object. For converting from an object language such as

C++, this is not an issue, because the application is already implemented as objects within each source file.

8.3.8 Converting C Function Prototypes to Method Prototypes

This step applies only to procedural languages such as C. In conversion of each source file into a class, C functions must be turned into Java methods within the new Java class. This is a simple process and requires only minor syntax changes.

8.3.9 Focusing on Conversion, Not Object-Oriented Design

Even though Java is an object-oriented programming language, developers should not get caught up in creating a pure object-based system during the conversion of a C application. The focus should be on converting to Java technology. If a company has a well-architected system written in a procedural language that is being converted to Java technology, little advantage will be gained and a lot of confusion will be added by introducing object design during the conversion.

8.3.10 Incorporating Java's String Class

This step has a major impact on the system. The Java String class is one of the strengths of the Java language. In many business systems, custom, complex C/C++ code for performing string manipulation can be replaced by simple, easy-to-comprehend calls to the Java String class.

8.3.11 Incorporating Java's Date Class

Business systems frequently perform date manipulations. In many cases, legacy systems have custom infrastructure for storing and manipulating dates. In the Java language, date manipulation has been made simple. Complex, custom date code can be replaced by simple method calls to the Java Date class.

8.3.12 Converting Structures into Classes

In C programs, data is passed from module to module in data structures. The easiest way to convert these structures is through a Java class that preserves the concept of structures. A C structure can be implemented by creating a Java class with externally accessible fields and no methods. This step is simple for the conversion team to perform and is necessary in order to convert the C application.

8.3.13 Converting the Execution Architecture to the Java Language

Execution architectures are responsible for layering the business application of complex technology concepts. Just as in the case with the business logic, a clean architecture is much simpler to convert than a poorly written one. After the architecture functions have been converted, the application programs will need to be converted to use the new architecture's Application Programming Interfaces (APIs).

8.3.14 Executing the Java Compiler

The final step tests to see how successful the conversion process has been. The Java compiler will do a thorough job of verifying the new code and pointing out programming errors. Successfully compiling a converted application does not guarantee a successful conversion, but it is a strong sign that the conversion process is working.

8.4 Converting Business Systems to Java

The following two examples demonstrate the feasibility of converting existing systems to Java technology. In the *via* World Network example, application code was converted from C and COBOL. In the second example, a PowerBuilder application was converted to the Java language. Both were successful conversions and, because the project teams were converting from well-written systems, were relatively free of problems.

8.4.1 *via* World Network Conversion

The *via* World Network team performed a conversion of several C and COBOL modules totaling approximately 50,000 lines of complex business logic. The logic determined the price of an airline ticket, a complex business process. The original modules were written with consistent coding standards, and most of the technical complexity was hidden beneath an underlying architecture. If these modules had not been built cleanly, *via* World Network would probably not have undertaken the task of performing the conversion.

Before beginning the conversion, *via* World Network's management team requested assurances that the conversion would be successful. To determine the viability of the conversion, *via* World Network first converted a single, simple module. About 300 lines of a C program were converted manually, line by line. It took several tries and many abortive compilations, but after a day of work, the module compiled successfully. Unfortunately, the program did not have sufficient functionality to perform a test. However, reflecting on the complexity of the converted code and the lessons learned, *via* World Network believed that converting the rest of the 50,000 lines of code was feasible.

Before the major conversion took place, the technical team created a tool that could be used by developers to perform the simplest conversion steps. Most of the conversion steps were simple syntax changes from C to Java. Less than one week was spent building a simple tool. Tool development stopped at this point, because it was determined that it would take longer to create a robust tool than to convert the rest of the applications manually.

After the tool had been created, a detailed document explaining how to convert a legacy module was written. The document detailed the conversion steps previously described. Through these straightforward steps, the developers were guided in converting more than 90 percent of the applications.

In the next step, a developer converted one of the modules as a test of the conversion process. By performing a single conversion, *via* World Network was able to make an estimate of the time required to convert all 50,000 lines of code. After the conversion workplan had been established, a small team consisting of approximately ten developers was assigned to the task. They were given a one-week training course in the basics of the Java language and shown how to perform the conversion. After the course, they began the conversion.

What was interesting about the conversion team was that none of the developers had prior knowledge of the Java language, only a few knew C, and all were new employees with little or no programming experience. Despite this lack of development knowledge, they were able to convert all 50,000 lines of code successfully. The process was time-consuming because every line of code had to be rewritten, but few unexpected issues arose during the conversion.

The problems that were encountered occurred because the new system had not been based on a complete architecture. The new execution architecture for the Java application had been designed and much had been created, but there were still pieces to complete. This caused delays, because some details were not yet known about the new execution architecture. Once the new Java architecture had been completely defined, a little rework was required on the converted modules. Overall, however, the architecture issues added less than 5 percent to the total overall time budget.

One direction the team followed was to convert C modules directly to the Java language but to convert COBOL modules first to C and then to the Java language. This was done from concern that a conversion from COBOL to the Java language would be too complex. As it turned out, this was a false assumption, and the conversion took longer than necessary. Even though converting from COBOL to Java would have been more difficult than converting from C to Java (because the syntax of C is closer to Java), it still would have saved time to convert straight from COBOL to Java.

At the end of the *via* World Network conversion, all modules had to be thoroughly retested. This was an area for which the project had not been adequately budgeted. Whereas the conversion went smoothly and did not take longer than planned, the complete retesting of applications consumed much more time than anticipated. The lengths of time required to convert and test modules relative to the original development time are shown in Table 8.1.

Table 8.1   *via* World Network conversion metrics

Time to build original module:	X	
Time to test original module:	Y	
Time to convert module to Java:	1/4	X
Time to test converted module:	3/4	Y

For example, a module that originally took forty days to code and twenty days to test took the project only ten days to convert and fifteen days to retest. These metrics were consistent across all of the modules the team converted. An important point to consider is that skilled programmers are required to build modules from scratch, but *via* World Network successfully used new developers to perform the conversion.

The conversion was considered successful for the following reasons.

• The converted system successfully executed in production.

• The conversion did not require expensive, experienced application developers.

• The experienced developers were able to focus on designing new parts of the system.

8.4.2 Customer Sales Support Conversion

The second conversion involved a complex GUI application written in Power-Builder. The existing PowerBuilder application was a powerful tool for customer sales support. It had been deployed on multiple client engagements, but because the application was marketed to more clients, a Java version became a key buyer value.

To create a Java prototype as a proof-of-concept exercise, a team of technical programmers studied the PowerBuilder application and created a step-by-step process to convert PowerBuilder to the Java language. The process was divided into the following categories.

- Convert application windows

- Convert global functions

- Convert global structures

- Convert user objects

- Convert data windows

- Convert stored procedures

Despite not having significant PowerBuilder experience, the Java programmers were able to create a successful conversion process. The process was then used by a group of PowerBuilder developers who did not know Java. After several hundred days of conversion work, the core functionality had been converted and was demonstrated to potential customers. Once again, the conversion of an existing system to the Java language was a success.

The times required to convert from PowerBuilder to the Java language are shown in Table 8.2. The PowerBuilder conversion took slightly longer than the C conversion because of the degree to which PowerBuilder syntax differed from Java syntax.

Table 8.2   PowerBuilder conversion metrics

Time to build original module:	X	
Time to test original module:	Y	
Time to convert module to Java:	4/10	X
Time to test converted module:	3/4	Y

8.5 Summary

By means of two examples, this chapter has described a process and guidelines for the successful conversion of existing systems to the Java language. It is important to study the existing system carefully to ensure that it is both based on well-designed architecture and well written. If a company decides to move forward with a conversion, it should begin with a structured approach using the steps outlined. If this is done correctly, the company can have a successful conversion and leverage the benefits of a Java-based system. If a conversion is done incorrectly, the risks to the business include budget overruns and a system that is never successfully converted. Key considerations in converting existing systems to the Java language are as follows.

- Most business systems require costly and time-consuming upgrades sometime during their lifecycles.

- The most successful and least expensive conversions begin with a "clean" or well-written existing system.

- A structured approach should be developed and used when converting legacy systems.

- There are several advantages of converting existing systems to Java, but they must be weighed against the costs of conversion.

- Java's similarity to C and C++ makes conversions from these languages relatively straightforward.

- Conversion of application code to Java takes significantly less time than building the original system. The time required to test the converted system may be similar to the amount of time spent in the original application build.

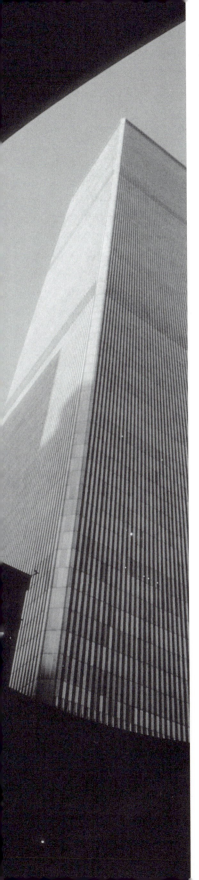

CHAPTER NINE

Managing a New Technology

9.1 Leveraging a New Technology

In the case studies used in this book, businesses have achieved a new level of competitive advantage through the use of Java technology. In each of these cases, the risks of a new technology were outweighed by the opportunities Java computing presented. For each of these companies, the risks involved in the use of Java technology were significant, including failure to obtain skilled resources, vendor support, development tools, and integration with third-party products. For companies to use a new technology such as Java successfully, a risk management strategy must be developed and executed. This chapter examines the risks of leveraging Java technology and outlines a sample risk management strategy.

9.2 Java's Rise in Popularity

In late 1995, the popularity of and interest in Java technology exploded. Java technology was the hottest new technology and the interest was tremendous. At first, curious developers had fun with Java programs, playing with the new language. Shortly thereafter, companies began looking at Java development as a possible solution to the problem of developing new business systems that leveraged the Internet. Soon, interest in Java technology grew to include investment by corporations. Companies began using the Java language on projects and began investing time and money in incorporating Java technology into their business system development plans.

Most new technologies follow an evolution in which they first are used by the technology sector and then filter into the business sector. The difference with Java technology was the speed at which the evolution took place. Under usual circumstances, creators of new technology have years from the time they introduce a new technology until it has been adopted by the mainstream business community. With Java technology, the transformation occurred over only a few months. In less than half a year (late 1995 to early 1996), Java went from obscurity to a technology in the limelight.

Meanwhile, Sun Microsystems had only a handful of people maintaining and developing the Java language. Many companies were interested, but Sun Microsystems had few resources to support them. At the time Java technology caught on, Sun Microsystems was not prepared for the deluge of interest.

Sun Microsystems tried to recover, but the flood of interest overtook the company. There were more requests for assistance than the company could handle. To support the budding technology, Sun Microsystems created an entire organization, JavaSoft, to develop and support Java computing. This organization was formed in early 1996 with a few developers from the company. Once formed, the new organization quickly began hiring additional people.

One of the new hires was a JavaSoft marketing representative. This marketing representative told the authors of this book an interesting story that put into perspective the level of interest in Java technology and how difficult it was for JavaSoft to keep up.

After joining the JavaSoft team, the representative was tasked with spreading the word about Java. Getting the word out about Java technology was easy because everyone in the industry was talking about it, but helping to answer questions and taking time to explain the future direction of Java was difficult because there were thousands of companies trying to get information from a small marketing team. To help get the word out more quickly, JavaSoft held conferences in several countries. The marketing representative made his presentations in front of thousands of people from around the world. Usually there was the opportunity for the audience to ask questions. After the questions were cut short because of time constraints, the session would end. After the session, people would mob him to ask more questions. If he tried to walk away, people would follow him. Even when he stopped in the restroom, people followed him in and continued to ask for information. There were just too many people trying to understand Java technology and too few resources.

A technical support person from JavaSoft also told Java technology stories to this book's authors. He said there were several thousand companies asking for help with Java implementations. Those companies called, wrote, sent e-mails—did whatever they could to get assistance. Literally thousands of companies were asking, demanding, and begging for direct assistance with their Java projects. Just responding to the requests was almost more than the Java support team could manage. Responding to these challenges, JavaSoft made available in 1997 several support programs with varying levels of support for corporate customers.

Although the stories from 1996 are now ancient history (in Internet time), they provide insight into the interest in Java technology and the subsequent level of support to expect from Sun and from other high-technology companies. When thousands of corporations, individuals, and educational institutions ask for assistance, rarely will a technology company dedicate resources at little or no cost. Ensuring adequate technology support assistance is just one example of the problems that have to be managed when working with a new technology such as Java.

9.3 Challenges in Using a New Technology

Despite the ever-increasing pace of new technology releases, it still takes years for a technology to become established and stabilized. Java technology suffers from growing pains that should not have been unexpected. The following issues combine the lessons learned from building the Java solutions found in the case studies and are likely to be issues other companies will face as well. Over time, many of these challenges will be reduced or eliminated, but until then, they must be taken into account when deciding whether or not to build a Java-based business system.

9.3.1 Don't Depend on Vendors to Come to the Rescue

As apparent from the stories told here, even JavaSoft has had difficulties in supporting the thousands of companies that have had questions or have needed assistance with Java technology. Obviously the number of available customer support representatives is limited. As organizations such as JavaSoft have matured, so has their customer support for Java. If a company is depending on

JavaSoft or another vendor for technology assistance and is expecting to pay little or nothing for this help, the company should carefully consider the viability of such a strategy.

9.3.2 Development Tools Are Emerging

Development tools for other computer languages have had years to mature. For Java applications, development tools are still in the process of being built. As of early 1998, the tools had improved drastically but were still behind the state of the art in other integrated development environments.

Any company interested in using Java technology should be prepared to take a step backward in the usability and capability of application development tools. For more information on this topic, see Chapter 20.

9.3.3 Integration with Existing Products

When a company is developing a large business system, it is wise to leverage existing products as much as possible. Companies have significant investments in software that they want to continue to use. Examples include integration of relational databases, communications products, billing systems, reservations systems, and human resource systems.

Most products available on the market today provide interfaces that allow C and C++ programs to integrate easily. In many cases, these interfaces do not exist for Java programs. Until these third-party vendors enhance their products to integrate with Java technology, companies will be required to build custom interfaces, which is a difficult, time-consuming process requiring skilled personnel.

A company considering Java will have to determine what, if any, third-party products will be integrated into its system. Each product must be evaluated to determine its compatibility with Java technology. If there is no Java interface to the product, the company will be required to create C or C++ interfaces with the product to integrate it into the rest of the Java system. This is not an impossible task, but it adds complexity and risk to the overall project.

9.3.4 There Are Still Bugs in Java

The JavaSoft team has done an excellent job of stabilizing the Java technology, and vendors creating Java runtimes have successfully implemented the Java standards. However, as for any new technology, not all of the kinks have been ironed out, especially in the more complex computing functions of Java. The intent here is not to identify the known bugs in Java, but to point out that they exist and will continue to exist as they would with any maturing technology.

There are several ways to address a suspected bug in the Java implementation. One way is to raise the issue to JavaSoft and work with JavaSoft to determine how to work around or resolve the problem. A second strategy is to have a close alliance with a technology company that has significant Java experience. Although the number of such companies is growing, it is important to look carefully at the work these companies have done to make sure that it is in line with the type of Java work needed. A third alternative is to build Java skills in house. If this alternative is chosen, it is best to start with C or C++ developers on the team and to implement Java projects in stages of increasing Java complexity.

9.3.5 Java Skills Are Scarce

Knowledge about technology is generally gained through education and experience. Because Java is an emerging technology, hiring those experienced in Java programming will be a challenge until educational institutions have implemented widespread Java training and until corporate use of Java has become commonplace.

Based on interviews with recent college graduates and university professors in 1996 and 1997, Java's adoption began in 1996 and will grow during the rest of the 1990s. The average college graduate should be expected to have some knowledge of Java but no significant implementation experience, because languages such as C and C++ still permeate computer science programs and will continue to do so for years to come (COBOL is still heavily taught at many campuses).

As for on-the-job training, few companies have been using Java technology long enough for a significant number of developers to have gained in-depth knowledge. The best option for a company that has decided to develop Java applications is to build skills internally. This is especially true for companies with strong C or C++ experience. For these companies, the development of Java skills will happen quickly, because the C/C++ developers should easily grasp Java concepts.

9.3.6 There Are Few Large Java Business Systems

One of the first common-sense actions a company takes when considering a new technology is to research other companies and projects that have built systems using the new technology. For a new technology, this can quickly become a "catch-22" situation, because everyone is waiting for someone else to "blaze the trail." Although Java technology will also be in this situation for a period of time, it will emerge more quickly than most technologies. The key is knowing when to strike. Is there enough experience, or should the company wait six months to let the market mature?

Any company doing research to assess the maturity of Java should first determine the target experience level it is seeking. Is it one, three, or ten case studies of Java implementations similar to the one under consideration? Having this objective in mind before doing the research will help track the evolution of Java technology and its level of appropriateness for the company's objectives.

Sites to review when determining Java's maturity include Gamelan (www.gamelan.com) and JavaSoft (www.javasoft.com). Both of these Web sites have numerous examples of successful Java implementations.

9.4 Java Risk Management

Java technology presents many attractive features that make it a powerful tool in developing and deploying commercial business systems. The biggest challenge to successful implementation of a large-scale Java system is having the foresight to anticipate and prepare for challenges along the way. By taking an incremental approach to developing a business system, key risks are identified early on, assumptions are tested early, and expensive rework can be avoided.

The key steps in a risk management approach focus on the early identification of technology weaknesses and rapidly adapting to these challenges. The key steps are as follows.

- Weigh the advantages of using Java technology against its risks.

- Define the underlying technology requirements and those areas requiring custom integration.

- Prototype the technology implementation.

- Begin development with a pilot set of developers.

9.4.1 Weigh Advantages against Risks

Before moving forward for the first time in constructing a business system with Java technology, a company should perform an extensive study of the pros and cons. Once a complex project has successfully delivered a Java system, business developers will understand many of the challenges and the resulting risks will be lessened for all future systems. Key decision points within the analysis that favor Java technology are listed below.

- Business requirements dictate a high degree of integration or usage of Internet technologies.

- There is a past history of successful C/C++ client/server implementation.

- The deployment of the system will be done to multiple platforms.

- The business system is strategic in nature and will be used for more than five years.

Decision points that do *not* favor the use of Java include the following.

- The business system is complex and mission-critical and must be deployed within six months.

- Significant integration with legacy C/C++ application code must be performed in order to deploy the business application successfully.

- Existing third-party software development packages meet the needs of the business system.

The results of this review may clearly indicate whether Java technology or a more mature alternative is the best choice. If the decision is not clear, Java technology is probably not the right tool to choose.

9.4.2 Identify Custom Technology Integration Requirements

Once it has been decided that Java technology is appropriate for a business system, an evaluation must be made to determine the technology infrastructure requirements. Until the technology matures, a Java business application will require more custom infrastructure to be successful. For example, early Java applications had to make use of C routines to call relational databases. Calling the relational databases required custom integration between the Java applications and the C routines. As more vendors support Java language access to their products, the need for custom integration will decrease. For example, the advent of the JDBC has eliminated the need for custom C code to access relational databases.

By identifying the custom integration requirements for the business system, a direct relationship to the risks and costs a company will incur can be determined. The more custom integration required, the higher the costs and risks.

9.4.3 Prototype the Technology Implementation

An early technology prototype is an important step for ensuring the viability of the proposed Java infrastructure. This prototype should test the integration of all the primary custom infrastructure and third-party software products. This testing will provide an early determination of whether or not the initial estimates of risk and cost were accurate.

9.4.4 Begin Development with a Pilot Set of Developers

For large-scale systems development requiring 20 or more developers, it is important to test business application development with a small pilot group. This step is another critical checkpoint that helps to avoid costly rework or delays in development owing to inadequacies in Java development tools. Once the pilot development project has been completed, the productivity of application developers and the tool improvements they require will be fully understood. When this information is known, steps can be taken to facilitate efficient and effective application development for the full-scale development project.

9.5 A Pioneer's Challenges

via World Network began building a Java system in early 1996 and was a pioneer in the use of Java technology to develop a mission-critical business system. *via* World Network encountered a number of challenges, including:

- A usable graphical application debugging tool

- A lack of experienced vendor support

- Performance of the Java applications

- Complexity of on-line programming for business application developers

- Integration of Java technology with third-party products

- Timely releases of new versions of Java technology

- A lack of Java-based business system examples

The first major hurdle encountered by the development team was the lack of a usable graphical debugger. This slowed down development but did not halt it, because developers found alternative methods of debugging their applications.

In this case, early identification of the problem with pilot developers provided time to develop standard tools for assisting the full development team.

The next obstacle was a lack of experienced support from vendors in the area of Java technology. Working with vendors to help address the key Java technology challenges allowed the vendors an opportunity to focus their assistance. By focusing on areas requiring custom integration, the project identified appropriate technology vendors and required support.

Early in the technology prototyping phase, the team realized that the performance of Java applications would not meet the needs of the business application. Transactions were taking too long to be processed by the core business logic, all of which was written in Java technology. Through the assistance of JavaSoft, the runtime of the Java application was improved to a point where users were experiencing acceptable response times.

The Abstract Window Toolkit (AWT) in Java provides the functions for implementing GUI functionality across multiple platforms. AWT in its earliest form was complex and had a number of issues. Early prototyping led to the conclusion that this layer of Java software should be shielded from developers to minimize the challenges developers would incur. The use of AWT should be carefully reviewed to ensure that the complexity and issues in its implementation do not lead to delays in development.

Another challenge discovered during technology prototyping was the integration of Java technology with C-based software products. A good example of this conflict can be found between the database vendor's product for accessing their databases through the C language and the Java runtime environment. After weeks of investigating a problem (with help from JavaSoft and the database vendor), a low-level incompatibility between the two products was discovered. This incompatibility is an example of the incomplete integration of a new technology with established third-party products.

As with many new technologies, JavaSoft was not able to release the latest version of Java technology on schedule. The original date for the release of a new version of Java (Release 1.1) was targeted for late summer 1996. Three months after the original release date, an early release copy was received, but it was too slow to be run in production. It was not until early 1997 that Java 1.1 was released in a production mode.

A final complication for this 1996 pioneering project was the lack of examples within the industry to provide guidance and support. Because Java technology was so new, few other major business systems had been built in Java. The project was positioned with no experienced resources. As Java implementations mature, this challenge will diminish; until then, each project must gauge the current level of industry support for Java development and whether or not it is at an appropriate level for the business.

9.6 Summary

Most of the challenges encountered in the early use of Java technology for building business systems were not inherent to Java as much as they were characteristic of a new technology. Although the use of Java technology can result in significant competitive advantage, the risks inherent in a new technology must be managed. A company must examine the advantages offered by the new technology, weigh the benefits those advantages could potentially offer against the risks of using a new technology, and make a decision. Key risks to manage in the early adoption of Java as a platform for building business systems include the following.

- Despite the many advantages of Java computing, there are risks resulting from the emerging nature of the technology.

- Java technology is popular. Because of the extreme interest in the technology, companies must carefully plan and implement a strategy of support from technology vendors.

- Java development tools are emerging and may not be equal (in terms of features and functionality) to development tools for other languages currently in use by the company.

- The integration of third-party products, especially those based on C/C++, may be a challenge as vendors begin to adopt Java technology. Such integration requires significant skilled resources if performed internally.

- Owing to the pace of its acceptance and release cycle, companies should accept and plan for challenges in the Java implementation. Although these problems can be overcome, they will result in some delays in application development and will require skilled resources.

- Deep Java skills are scarce. As Java technology is adopted by more and more companies, the skill base will increase but the demand will still be great. A company should carefully consider where it will obtain the necessary skills to complete its project.

• Java technology is well suited for building and deploying business systems; however, the overall experience in this area is immature when compared with technologies such as C, C++, and COBOL. This will result in application development delays as companies are forced to learn from experience in evolving their initial Java-based business applications.

• Companies should develop a risk management strategy to mitigate the risks of using Java technology and ensure successful development of Java-based business systems.

CHAPTER TEN

Is Java Right for Everyone?

10.1 Is Java Right for the Business?

During the initial release and development stages of a technology, only a limited number of companies have the ability successfully to leverage the technology in order to develop innovative and visionary systems. These companies accept the fact that they are on the cutting edge, relish it, and fill the gaps in technology with "home grown" tools and assets. When building mission-critical business systems, companies should carefully consider the risks associated with Java technology's immaturity and lack of third-party product support. In addition, some companies are not ready to adopt a new technology such as Java because of their relative inexperience with technologies that support Java development, such as large-scale client/server operations. Technology maturity and related technology experience are relative measures and are inexact descriptions. The purpose of this chapter is to identify key maturity and experience issues that will help a company determine whether or not it is ready to use Java technology to build mission-critical systems.

10.2 Technology Challenges

Leveraging Java technology to build business applications may result in corporate competitive advantage and reduced systems development and support costs. While these are compelling advantages in favor of Java development, there are a number of situations in which these advantages do not outweigh the risks to the business. Many companies have significant systems technology investments that, in almost all cases, are not based on the Java language. In addition, these companies have employees trained in the use of non-Java technologies. Java development may be able to leverage significant portions of the existing development tools and technical training, but some conversion and retraining will be required. The advantages of Java technology must be weighed against these costs.

In other cases, companies have projects that are currently being developed with non-Java technologies. Should these projects be halted or at least delayed to leverage Java technology? Depending on the state of the project, the cost of refitting the overall solution with Java technology is an important consideration to weigh against the expected benefits.

A final area of concern is in the use of Java technology for mission-critical systems. In the *via* World Network case study, Java technology demonstrated the ability to be the platform for a system that was highly complex with more than 15,000 function points. Because this system delivered *via* World Network's travel management services, the successful development and deployment of this system was absolutely critical to the company's success. Before launching a mission-critical project such as *via* World Network's, a company should carefully consider its experience and the state of Java before "betting the business." Although Java technology can deliver tremendous benefits to the business, it can neither overcome a lack of sufficient experience by a company nor be removed from the fast-paced and rapidly changing world of Internet technologies. Java experience and the pace of technology change are factors that each company should consider when investigating the advisability of building Java-based business systems.

10.3 Before Using Java, Ask These Questions

The following questions help determine whether or not the maturity of Java technology matches a company's unique culture and situation. Technology maturity is a relative term: a mature technology to one company will be described as emerging by another company. These questions define what is meant by technology maturity in the context of an individual company.

• How important to the company is it to be a technology leader?

• Have developers been experimenting with Java applications?

- Do the appropriate third-party products exist to meet business requirements?

- Does the company have a culture of "filling the gaps" with new technologies?

- Does the company have the fortitude and investment capacity to be working in a fast-paced, rapidly changing environment?

- Does the company have a "green field" or new project?

10.3.1 Technology Leadership

Java technology can weave together the power of the Internet, Web browsers, intranets, and multiplatform computing. This is a technology that can help companies meet their business objectives, improve service and product delivery, and leapfrog competition. Along with the opportunity is the risk that Java computing will become a research and development budget sinkhole without delivering a competitive or revenue advantage for the company. The answer here lies in corporate history. Over the last ten years, has the corporation been known internally and/or externally as a technology opportunist where business success has been linked to new and innovative uses of technology? If the answer to this question is no, the company should take a path of building skills, demonstrating prototypes, and developing technology partnerships before undertaking the development of a mission-critical Java application.

10.3.2 Have Developers Been Experimenting?

Are there examples within the company on either Internet or intranet Web servers where Java applications or demonstrations have been written? If so, the people who have worked on these applications are the best starting point for building a Java team. If no examples can be found, this is a strong indicator that the company does not have the skills and infrastructure in place to deliver a critical business system.

10.3.3 A "Filling-the-Gaps" Culture

Java technology is rapidly evolving and quickly gaining third-party product support. Despite Java technology's rapid evolution, many companies will find that not all of their existing third-party product suppliers have full Java support. Does the company have a strong group of developers that can use Java technology and yet "fill the gaps" in the integration of third-party product solutions?

10.3.4 Third-Party Product Support

Third-party products are critical to delivering economical solutions that meet business requirements. Java is an evolving technology, and third-party products can minimize risk and maximize the opportunity to build skill and capability in Java. Attempting to build complex, critical business systems in Java without a partner or third-party products (such as database access, GUI tools, etc.) will lengthen the delivery time and increase the risk of project failure as a result of unexpected technology challenges and problems.

10.3.5 A Fast-Paced, Rapidly Changing Environment

By its very nature, Java technology is closely associated with rapidly evolving environments. Java is changing and will continue to change not only in its implementation but also in the level and capability of third-party product support. While Java development can help a corporation deliver critical business systems, the decision to use Java technology should be one that consciously recognizes Java's dynamic and evolving nature. Because of this rapidly evolving nature, new Java technology solutions are constantly being released. To maximize its use of Java, the company should stay abreast of these developments and make use of them as appropriate. This leads to additional research costs and potentially to rework expenses.

Delivering a business system requires that decisions be made on the basis of the best information available. Invariably, at some future time, this choice will be analyzed and reanalyzed with 20/20 hindsight. With hindsight, the choice of using Java technology and the third-party product decisions will look different. Does the company have the executive management backing to "stay the course" despite the changing nature of the technology?

10.3.6 Does the Company Have a "Green Field" Project?

The best place to start with Java development is on a project in which very few technology decisions have been made. Attempting to leverage Java technology for a project that was planned on the basis of other technologies can have the following undesirable effects.

- Delays in the project while Java technology is analyzed.

- Wrath and lack of support from supporters of the alternative technology.

- Misunderstanding of the impacts of changing a technology platform midstream and radical underestimation of the cost of switching to Java development.

- Loss of executive management buy-in through revisiting of technology decisions.

Java development is a significant departure from other technologies and tools used to deliver critical business systems. Starting with a "green field" project in which significant technology decisions have not yet been made provides the opportunity to build on Java technology as it was designed to be used, rather than substituting it in a system that was not originally intended to leverage Java capabilities.

10.4 Does the Business Have the Right Skills?

To realize the benefits of using Java technology, the risks of unexpected technology problems have to be managed. Many of these unexpected challenges are closely related to the technology that works with or supports Java development. The following are the fundamental technology skills a business should have in place when building a complex business system with Java technology.

- *Client/server technology.* Java computing was designed to leverage client/server technology. The Java language's powerful networking and user interface capabilities are well suited for a client/server deployment of a critical business system; however, client/server systems are complex to manage, control, and deploy. By their nature and the state of the market, multiple vendors must be chosen for operating system, client hardware, server hardware, database, and networking technology. Choosing vendors is just the start, and the products will have to be installed, integrated, and operated. Choosing Java computing as a base for delivering a complex, critical business system should be done only when the company has the ability to implement and support client/server technologies.

- *Object-oriented computing technology.* For more than ten years, object-oriented computing has been hailed as the next great advancement in development computer systems. Unfortunately, this technology has not fully delivered on the hype, especially in the creation and implementation of business systems. The reasons for this failure include the complexity and the coordination and training requirements for effective delivery of object-oriented systems. The Java language is object-oriented and is an improvement over C++ in its syntax and adherence to object-modeling theory. The traps and pitfalls object-oriented systems have been prone to are very real risks in building a Java-based system. Companies should have significant object experience and should be skilled in implementing object-based systems before using Java technology to build a large, complex critical business system.

- *Intranet technology.* Using the definition that an "intranet" is a corporate network based on TCP/IP network protocols, intranet technology is critical to developing and deploying internal Java systems. TCP/IP is the "communication language" of the Internet and is the base technology responsible for file transfers, remote access of systems, and the transmission of Web pages. TCP/IP is also the de facto network protocol for implementing client/server systems. Although IBM mainframe versions of Java technology exist (where TCP/IP has only recently been gaining acceptance), Java technology is firmly rooted in TCP/IP. Without the skills and experience in developing and operating a corporate intranet, the extent of a Java-based system's deployment will be limited to corporate local area networks.

- *Web technology.* Web technology includes HTML-based documentation, Web servers, and Web browsers. These technologies are critical to successful Java systems because they are the environment in which most Java systems are deployed. Java applets are deployed to Web servers and are referenced by HTML documents. As an HTML document is accessed, a Web browser also loads and executes the referenced Java applet. If a company has not deployed Web technology, the ability for the company to leverage the full potential of Java technology will be limited.

- *Internet technology.* "Does the company have a Web site?" is a question that should be asked early on. If Java development is intended to be used as a tool for reaching customers or suppliers over the Internet, the corporation should have significant experience in the performance, availability, and security issues related to the Internet. A solid Java business system may not be successful over the Internet if the company cannot meet the challenges of security, performance, and availability.

10.5   Acquiring the Right Skills

The following three steps will help to build the skills and infrastructure needed for developing Java-based business systems.

• *Build the related technology skills and infrastructure.* Internet, intranet, Web, object-oriented, and client/server skills are critical for successful deployment of Java-based systems. Most companies have at least a subset of these skills and need to focus on one or two areas. Training seminars, conferences, and industry publications are powerful tools for building the raw skills necessary for successfully implementing Java-based systems. These skills should then be leveraged to develop prototypes and working infrastructures that demonstrate and deliver these technologies in a business setting.

• *Find a "green field" business application.* By beginning with a new application for which no decision on a programming language has been made, the design team will focus on leveraging Java computing rather than using it to replace an alternative technology. When Java is used as a replacement technology, the risk is in changing horses in the middle of the stream. Time and risk increase, because the focus is on replacing the technology rather than implementing the business solution.

• *Develop in an iterative fashion.* As the system is being built, exciting technical skills will be acquired; however, remember to maintain the team's focus. Java technology may let business application developers become too enamored with the technology and lose sight of the business problem. Through an iterative development process, short-term business objectives can be identified that will keep the project on track.

The points above are general approaches to acquiring Java skills. Chapter 18 is an in-depth discussion of the strategies and approaches for developing Java skills within an existing application development organization.

10.6 Summary

Java technology is not for everyone. Java computing is a powerful technology that not only can deliver significant solutions to complex business challenges but also can help deliver competitive advantages. As with any powerful tool, Java technology can cause problems and headaches that outweigh the business advantages it delivers. It is important for companies to consider the following questions.

• Has Java technology matured to a point to which the company can successfully implement a Java-based business system? Six questions that will help a company determine if it is ready for Java-based business systems are:
  • How important to the company is it to be a technology leader?

- Have developers been experimenting with Java applications?
- Do strong third-party products exist to meet business requirements?
- Does the company have a culture of "filling the gaps" with new technologies?
- Does the company have the fortitude to be working in a fast-paced, rapidly changing environment?
- Does the company have a "green field" or new project?

- Does the company have the related technology skills and infrastructure to deliver, deploy, and operate a complex, critical Java-based business system? Experience and skills in five technology areas are critical to the successful implementation of Java-based business systems.
  - Client/server systems
  - Object-oriented development
  - Intranet technology
  - Web technology
  - Internet technology

- What's the best way to develop the right Java skills? The three steps a company must take to create the Java skill and experience necessary for building and deploying mission-critical Java applications are:
  - Building related skills
  - Leveraging a "green field" application
  - Developing iteratively

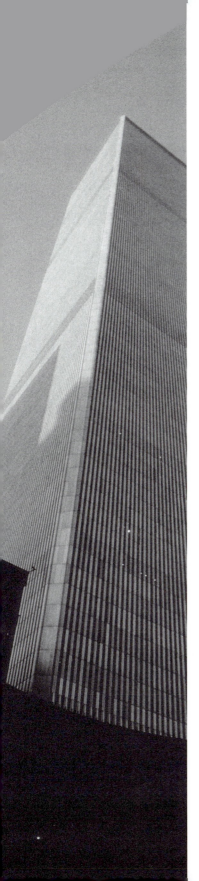

CHAPTER ELEVEN

Bridging Procedural and Object-Oriented Styles

11.1 Application Development Styles

In business application development there are primarily two techniques or styles that can be used to create software applications: procedural and object-oriented development. There are proponents of each type of programming, but many software development purists prefer object development, while most business systems have been and continue to be written in the more traditional procedural style.

Procedural development has been around since the beginning of computers. The two most common programming languages that follow this technique are COBOL and C. A procedural style simply means that lines of code are executed sequentially. To organize programs, modules or functions are created. Tracing the execution of procedural applications is straightforward, because the logic follows from one line to the next. Procedural code is generally broken into several source and definition files. Source files contain application logic, and definition files contain data definitions.

Object technology's promise is to develop systems that are easier to maintain and that promote more reuse of application code. Although several languages have been developed with object technology, a popular language for object development in business systems is C++. For many years, object development has been predicted to be the "silver bullet" in the software industry. Object technology was intended to revolutionize programming, bring a new level of productivity to developers, and generate robust, easy-to-maintain systems. The downside to object technology is its requirement for greater training and coordination than procedural system development.

There have been numerous cases where object technology has produced the benefits predicted. At the same time, there have been more cases (especially in business applications) where object technology has not yielded the predicted benefits and has resulted in cost overruns, delays, or cancellation of the project. In many cases, the use of object technology can be traced to a strong technology advocate. More than procedural proponents, object advocates are religious about using object technology and may pursue technical solutions at the expense of business requirements. An object advocate will give an eloquent, convincing argument as to why a company should use object technology. These arguments most often turn into reality when only a few, seasoned object experts are building the business system. A large team of more than 20 developers with limited object skills will have difficulty maintaining cohesion, coordination, and focus.

11.2　Objects Are Not for Everyone

Despite the widespread interest in object-oriented development, it has failed to revolutionize the software industry as expected. Some of the key reasons object-oriented development has not had the anticipated impact are as follows.

- A fine-grained object-oriented system is difficult to attain.

- Reuse is more difficult than most people believe.

- Most developers and existing systems are procedural.

11.2.1　Fine-Grained Object-Oriented Design Is Difficult to Attain

In a fine-grained object-oriented system, everything is an object. All code fits neatly into an object, the objects are logically constructed, and communication between objects is compact and easy to understand. To reach this level of granularity in a large-scale system, the design of the object-oriented system is revisited multiple times as each new feature or enhancement is added. As scope changes and the overall system design becomes more detailed, it is difficult to avoid continuous rewrites as lead designers attempt to preserve the purity of an object design.

To illustrate the difficulty of creating an object system from the ground up, consider what would happen in the following scenario. Ask the project's best object developer to create a fine-grained object design. Feed one requirement at a time and have the developer attempt to draw up an object design. As more features and requirements are added, two things happen: the design becomes very complex, and there is constant redesign as new, incongruent requirements are added. After a few hours of this task, the design will have evolved into a complex set of objects and interrelated rules for communication. If a design can become complex and incur redesign in a few hours with the best object developer on the project, imagine what would happen on a large project with less-talented object developers trying to create a fine-grained object system. Such inexperienced object developers would struggle even to agree on the definition of objects and how they should be interrelated.

This lesson does not apply to smaller projects requiring only a few developers, because scope can be quickly communicated and changed. When there are hundreds of developers, the attempt to create a pure object design can easily fail. Part of the solution may be forthcoming from the software industry. When large-grained objects, sometimes called components, are used, the complexity of objects can be reduced while still leveraging the benefits. Companies should not abandon the idea of using object programming, but they should be aware of its limitations. In large projects, a purely object-oriented design is a very difficult thing to achieve without the appropriate experience and personnel.

11.2.2 Reuse Is Difficult

The primary claimed benefit of object development is reuse. If objects are created with well-defined, clear, and easy-to-use interfaces, other developers will be able to leverage what already has been built rather than having to develop it from scratch. Reuse not only saves time and expense but also promotes consistency in the overall implementation of a business system.

The economies of reuse from object development are difficult to achieve. The following reasons provide an explanation of why reuse has not been the "silver bullet."

- *Companies cannot reuse their most complex logic.* Complex business logic typically is specific to only one part of the business, which causes the logic to be used only for its initial purpose. For example, the complex logic designed to identify a target customer market would not be used by a customer service system.

- *The business world is dynamic.* The business logic used to support a company today may not be appropriate tomorrow. Over time, this prevents a company from continuously reusing its existing code base.

- *The cost of reuse is high.* It takes time and money for developers to create clean interfaces to their objects and to document and publish those interfaces. It also takes developers time to search through another developer's objects to find reusable pieces. The time required to document and search for the right object is often more than the project's budget can afford.

- *Personnel turnover impacts reuse.* Personnel turnover within companies eats away at the knowledge of what is available and how to reuse it. The complexity of object development requires significant depth of knowledge about the design and implementation of the system. This knowledge comes best from having built the system in the first place. Once the original developers have left the company, their replacements do not have the original design and implementation knowledge to help make decisions regarding reuse.

- *Existing projects have been able successfully to share small objects such as date and string classes.* However, reusing small utility classes is not a big benefit to the company. The real benefit for companies lies in the reuse of major portions of business logic such as financial processing or customer sales support logic.

- *The larger the project, the harder it is to coordinate sharing of code.* As the size of the system grows, the number of objects grows. This makes effective reuse even more expensive and difficult.

- *Creating generic, reusable objects takes more time.* Reusable application objects are not specific to one problem and can be used in a variety of situations. Creating generic objects, however, takes more time and effort than developing single specific implementations—time that is often in short supply during the construction of large, complex business systems.

Because of the obstacles preventing reuse, object-oriented development loses one of its primary benefits. Companies should be careful not to be oversold on the reuse advantages of object development.

11.2.3 The Pervasiveness of Procedural Systems

The vast majority of business systems in use in the 1980s and 1990s have been procedural in nature. Usually written in COBOL or C programming languages, these systems perform essential and critical business functions and will not be replaced for many years. Owing to this existing legacy of procedural applications, most developers graduating from universities or already in the industry are procedural developers. Converting a procedural developer into an effective object developer is a costly task that does not always prove successful.

Most developers naturally think procedurally. They think in a statement-by-statement fashion. They can easily pick up a piece of procedural code and decipher its contents. Because of the simplicity, long history, and prevalence in education and business associated with procedural development, there are many more experienced procedural developers than object developers today.

As compared with procedural programming, object development is more complex. There are more features to deal with, there are more techniques to learn, and it is easier to create a poorly structured program. Experienced and expert object software developers are more difficult and expensive to obtain than procedural developers.

11.3 Combining Object-Oriented and Procedural Styles

To find the right balance, the differences between object-oriented and procedural development must be understood. One way of illustrating these differences is with an analogy involving two telephones. Object development is represented by a modern phone with complex features and functionality, whereas procedural development is represented by an older phone that supports nothing more than the placing of phone calls. Although the new phone has several advantages over the simpler one, there are problems with its use. The first challenge is in training old users to use all the new features. Over time it is discovered that of the many new features on the new phone, only a small percentage are ever used by callers, because the primary purpose of the phone was served by the original phone. The best approach is to take only the useful new features and combine them with the old model.

In many cases, the functions and features of object development far exceed the requirements of the business. Whereas some features are beneficial, others require too much training and planning to be used effectively. If the object techniques are not pushed too far, training can be successful. Object development ultimately breaks down to procedural statements. An object is just a collection of variables and functions. In its basic form, object development is not vastly different from procedural programming. Unfortunately, object development is often pushed to an extreme where inexperienced developers are responsible for complex object-oriented concepts. When procedural developers must create their own objects, define how "big" the objects are, and clearly define the objects' behaviors and interfaces, the level of system complexity rises exponentially. Building an object that will successfully interact with other objects in a large system is a daunting task for an inexperienced team of object developers. Even more complex is maintaining overall system stability when business requirements change.

As in the telephone analogy, one strategy is to take the best features of object development and combine them with the best features of procedural development to produce a powerful yet productive application development environment. An approach to creating a hybrid object/procedural environment is to designate talented object developers as the business system architects and to "hide" most of the object difficulties from the mainstream (or procedural) developers. By leveraging the most talented object developers, a framework for the rest of the team can be created. The best object developers will create a high-level system design that provides the rest of the team with the basic building blocks (in other words, common, reusable objects) to use in development. The majority of the developers are not burdened with object development details; rather, they are focused on creating a system that meets the business objectives. The majority of the business developers can concentrate less on technology implementation and more on functionality. Each developer is given a set of components or "large-grained" objects and develops procedurally within those objects. The resulting business system can leverage object-oriented development advantages at the "large-grained" object level. By isolating the design to a limited number of experienced object developers and by defining objects in a "large-grained" manner, the best features of both procedural and object technology can be realized.

11.4   Java Bridges the Two Styles

Even though the Java language is considered an object programming language, it can be used to bridge the gap between object and procedural development. For a project looking to build a business system leveraging object concepts and procedural experience, Java is an excellent choice for the following reasons.

- *The Java language is an object language and therefore has all of the object-oriented benefits.* Generally, everything that is done in existing object languages can be done in Java programming. In fact, many object experts believe that the Java language enforces object-oriented development rules better than C++.

- *The basic syntax of the Java language is similar to that of C and can be used to create C-like applications.* By coding procedurally inside a component framework provided by experienced object-oriented developers, Java applications look much like C programs. Procedural developers understand this approach quickly.

- *The Java language simplifies object concepts and syntax from C++.* The object concepts that are most difficult to comprehend have been simplified in the Java language. This makes the job easier for those developers trying to architect and develop the overall system as well as improve the learning curve for new developers.

Despite the advantages Java programming offers for building an object/procedural system, the most important thing for project developers to do is to design the system appropriately. The business system can be designed to leverage object concepts and technologies, but inexperienced object application developers should develop procedurally to minimize the risks of object development.

11.5 Example Java-Based Object/Procedural Systems

This section is based on the creation of multiple successful business systems built in Java using both experienced and inexperienced object developers. Even though these projects used Java, a strong object language, the business application developers coded procedurally and avoided the pitfalls of object-oriented development.

The *via* World Network project was comprised of approximately 50 application developers. Of the 50, only about five could be considered experienced object developers. Yet, despite this overall lack of experience, an object/procedural system was built with ease. This development was easy because it followed an overall object approach while allowing the developers with less object experience to code procedurally within frameworks developed by more experienced object developers. Procedurally trained developers new to the project were able to develop successful new applications after only three weeks of training. The component development approach allowed the developers to focus on understanding C/Java language differences rather than on learning object-oriented design and development.

A second project leveraged the skills developed within the *via* World Network system to convert an existing client/server system to Java. The original system had been built with a popular procedural-based tool, and all of the project's developers had been trained procedurally. By working closely with the business application developers, three experienced object developers created frameworks and tools to shield the developers with less object experience. The result was a highly successful project in which the original system was quickly and effectively migrated to the Java language by procedural developers.

A third project leveraged experienced object developers to lead a team of less-experienced developers in building a document management system for customer support. In this system, the inexperienced developers built application logic within components. These object-oriented components were maintained by experienced developers, which allowed the inexperienced developers to write procedural logic within the object-based shell during their first few weeks on the project.

At a high level, all three systems were designed with an object model in mind. Each function for the system was assigned a logical object, ensuring that each business operation was treated as an object. Each business object had a well-defined function and well-defined interfaces. Within each object, the developers coded in a procedural fashion. This allowed the system architects and lead developers to design the system in an object-oriented manner and then break up the logic into workable units. The developers coding the business logic were not involved in the overall object design and focused exclusively on the business objects they were assigned. By hiding a majority of object complexity from developers, the projects were able to leverage the existing procedural programming skills.

These projects would not have been able to meet aggressive budgets or timelines by using an object-oriented development strategy with their existing development organizations. These projects were able successfully to use a large group of procedural developers to create object-based systems in an object programming language. The Java language did not provide all of the answers, but it did ease the transition from strict procedural development to a hybrid object/procedural implementation.

11.6 Summary

Despite all of the hype surrounding object programming, the technology has its downfalls. It is easy to be drawn in by object advocates and lose sight of the dangers of a fine-grained object-oriented approach. For a business that has limited experience with objects, it is critical to find a middle ground between procedural and object development. This middle ground leverages existing procedural skills while taking advantage of object-oriented development concepts. Through several successful projects, Java technology has demonstrated itself to be a powerful tool that can be understood by procedural developers yet deliver on many of the promises of object technology. Key messages in using Java technology to bridge procedural and object-oriented systems are as follows.

- In the business world, procedural-based systems are older and more pervasive than object-based systems.

- Object-based systems are more difficult to build, but the promise of improved productivity, reusability, and maintainability is powerful.

- Java can be used to support either a procedural or an object approach.

- For companies with a significant base of procedural developers, an approach worth considering is building the system in a way that leverages elements of both procedural and object styles.

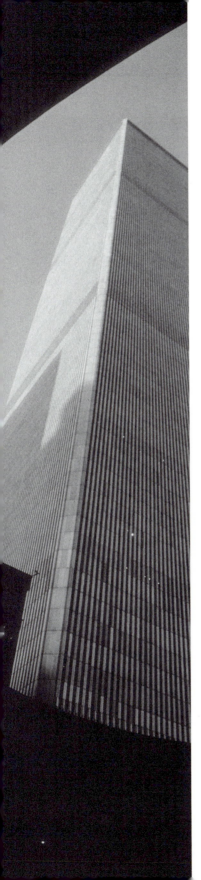

CHAPTER TWELVE

Building Execution Architectures

12.1 Execution Architectures

Developing large, complex business systems requires dozens if not hundreds of developers. Two ways of measuring the size and complexity of business systems development projects are by the amount of time (workdays) required to build the system and the number of function points (features) within the system. For this chapter, a large system is assumed to require the work of more than 20 developers for a year or be measured at more than 10,000 function points in complexity. The larger the system, the more difficult it becomes for developers to understand how their individual pieces fit into the overall puzzle. When a large systems development project is spread across many developers, companies try to divide the work into smaller, logically formed pieces. This process eases project management and coordination among developers. One of the primary dividing lines used in breaking apart the work is to separate the technology from the business function.

This approach divides team members into two groups: business function developers and technical developers. Business function developers focus on writing the business logic of the system, and technical developers focus on providing the underlying technology. This organization optimizes team performance by allowing team members to focus on either the business logic or the technology, but not both. Programmers focusing on business requirements tend to spend their time on two activities: understanding business requirements and turning these requirements into applications. The technology team members provide the technical framework and foundation on which the business logic resides, as shown in Figure 12.1.

The technical team determines the hardware and operating system platform of the system and also purchases and installs the equipment. After the hardware is in place, the technical team chooses which programming language to use, determines which development tools to purchase or build, and plans how the system will be maintained. Once development has begun, part of the technical team supports the functional developers when technical problems are encountered.

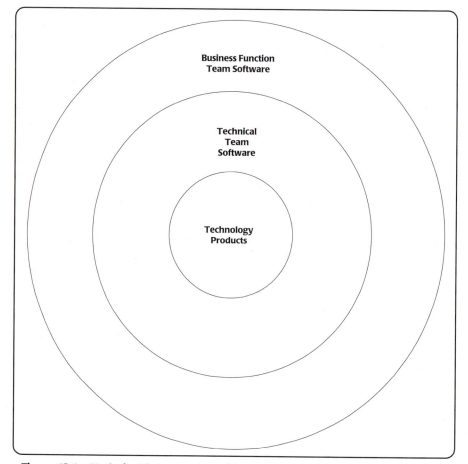

Figure 12.1   Technical framework and foundation

Another responsibility of the technical team is to provide software routines that simplify the use of technology for application developers. This software layer provided by the technology team hides technical details and saves time for business developers. This software is called an execution architecture (see Figure 12.2).

An execution architecture is a collection of software routines, tools, third-party products, programs, rules, templates, and standards that are configured or created by the technical team to simplify application development for the

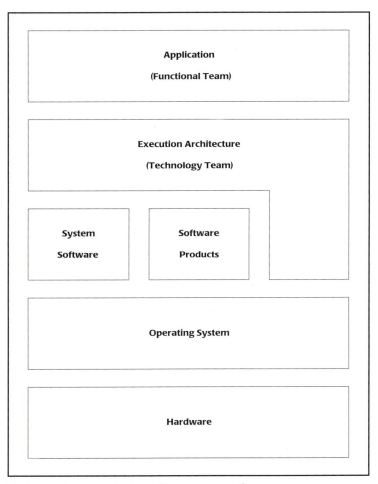

Figure 12.2   Execution architecture layer diagram

business function teams. The scope and size of the execution architecture depend on the needs of the business application. Areas that are commonly covered include:

- *Database access.* In the client/server world, making a call to the database requires several steps and an understanding of both the client and server sides of the database request. Building simple, robust, and efficient database access routines often can be leveraged across an entire project.

- *Network communication.* Network communication is a complex technical issue involving topics such as security, time-outs, retry, and platform dependencies. This is one of the most difficult areas to program correctly and is best left to the technical team members.

- *Common utilities.* Common utilities include programmatic constructs common to most applications. Examples of utilities include date routines, string routines, and sort routines. Building them into the architecture prevents the business team from building them for each application and allows the technical team to ensure that the basic common building blocks of the system are standardized and bug free.

- *File access.* Programming tasks as simple as file access are included in the execution architecture. The functional team should not be concerned with the physical locations of data, file permissions, or file corruption.

- *Error handling.* By creating a framework for error handling, establishing standards, and providing common error-handling routines, all applications in a system will be consistent and robust. It is not efficient for every developer of a system to create his or her own standards for error handling. Having a small team of technical developers study error handling within the project and determine the most comprehensive, easy-to-implement error-handling solution will provide a more robust final implementation.

- *GUI framework and widgets.* Programming constructs such as interwindow communication, window level validation, tabbing, folders, and other complex GUI structures are difficult to build. These functions should be built once and then provided to the team as a common set of routines. This approach also provides a consistent style to all GUI applications in a large system.

- *Memory management.* Memory management should be performed in the execution architecture. Without this feature in the architecture, programmers are forced to perform memory management that requires intensive work and often produces runtime errors. By standardizing and centralizing memory allocation within an execution architecture, the project creates a more robust application and saves time for the business function application developers.

This list of architecture components is by no means complete but provides examples of what is commonly included in an execution architecture. Each area in the list expands into a set of library routines, standards, and programming examples. Once complete, an execution architecture has the following characteristics.

- *Ease of understanding and use.* The main goal of the business developer is to understand the business requirements, not the technology. The execution architecture should be easy for even a new programmer to understand and use.

- *Simplicity and consistency.* The set of routines and standards should be kept to a minimum, requiring less learning and less code from the developers and enforcing more consistency across programs.

- *Stability.* As soon as possible, the interface between the application program and the execution architecture should be finalized. A stable environment will increase both the productivity of developers and their confidence in the underlying technology.

- *Good documentation.* Before an execution architecture is rolled out to programmers, it must be well documented. The documentation should explain the purpose of each function in the architecture, how to use each function, and what happens when it is called. On large development projects with new architecture and new developers, it makes sense also to hold a few training sessions to bring the development team up to speed with the features and functions of the execution architecture.

12.2 The Business Case

Before time and money are invested in the creation of an execution architecture, the business case of expected gains versus costs should be analyzed. Large development projects (those with more than 20 developers) generally realize significant benefits. These benefits occur through the increased efficiency of application developers. For large and small projects, the following list of advantages should be compared with the cost of building an execution architecture.

- *Increased productivity.* Business developers responsible for building the application save time in two ways. First, these developers use software layers provided by the technical team that are easy to use and hide technical details, which saves on time spent in learning the technology. The second way in which developers save time is through reuse. An execution architecture provides routines that are used hundreds, or even thousands, of times throughout the system.

- *More robust applications.* Focusing technically strong developers on the most technically difficult code creates a more robust application. Most functional developers do not have the expertise to solve deep technical challenges effectively and robustly.

- *Improved production operations.* Execution architectures enforce standards across all applications in a large business system, which eases production operations. For example, if database access for all applications is performed through simple routines provided by the execution architecture, the operations support is much more efficient than supporting several applications each with its own technique for database access. Centralized routines, standard coding practices, similar application frameworks, and a robust technical implementation make a system easier to operate.

- *Simpler application maintenance.* Creating a standard application framework through which all applications execute makes long-term maintenance easier. Consistency across applications allows for easier updates of the business logic for applications in a large system.

- *Insulation from technology changes.* By insulating the business application from the underlying technology, the logic interfacing with the underlying infrastructure is centralized. If the database software or operating system is upgraded, only the architecture has to change, not the application. Efficiencies in upgrades are realized because the architecture is generally less than 10 percent the size of the application.

- *Multiple project leverage.* If a company has more than one system to build, an execution architecture saves additional time and money through reuse. Business logic is typically specific for a particular project, but the underlying execution architecture is application independent. This independence allows a company to create a single execution architecture and reuse it across multiple development projects.

- *Operations management.* An execution architecture allows centralized support of metrics gathering, performance tuning, and debugging. As an example, having database access go through a single standard architecture routine provides the project resources with a single point for database access debugging and tuning.

12.3 The Downside of Execution Architectures

Execution architectures ultimately save in development costs and create more robust solutions, but there are disadvantages. Issues include:

- *Complexity.* It is very difficult to build a full-featured execution architecture. The team will require deep technical experience to build it correctly.

- *Expense.* Creating an execution architecture is a significant cost to a project. The cost will eventually be outweighed by the benefits, but it may be difficult to convince management of the rationale of an execution architecture given the necessary investment that must be made.

- *Time.* It generally takes months to create a working execution architecture. Before the architecture is functioning, it is difficult to begin development, which may be a delay that a project cannot accept.

- *Choices.* When a project team decides to build an execution architecture, it is faced with a dilemma in choosing the best solution. It undergoes a period of confusion as to the best technology to incorporate into the execution architecture. Once the project has begun, team members may question the validity of decisions. Always trying to justify the direction of the execution architecture and adjusting as necessary can be a costly mistake to the project and can prevent the architecture from ever being built.

12.4 Advantages of Java

Java technology is not an execution architecture, but it offers new tools and advantages over existing technologies. In languages such as C, C++, and COBOL, technology teams must build common utility functions, multithreading capabilities, network communication functions, and database access with little assistance. The capabilities inherent in Java development contribute significantly to the building of an execution architecture, reducing the build time and making the final implementation simpler and more robust. The advantages of using Java technology to build execution architectures for large system development projects are discussed in the following subsections.

12.4.1 No Memory Management

A function frequently built into C and C++ execution architectures is memory management. Problems with memory allocation and deallocation are common on large systems projects, especially those built in languages such as C and C++. The execution architecture manages the application's memory for several reasons: to reduce memory faults, ensure optimal usage, and ensure proper cleanup. Building a comprehensive memory management scheme not only is time-consuming but also does not guarantee success, because developers may use it incorrectly.

The Java programming language eliminates the need for an execution architecture to perform memory management. Java technology completely manages memory for the application. There are no memory faults and no improper memory deallocations.

12.4.2 Standard, Comprehensive Approach to Error Handling

An important characteristic of an execution architecture is that it enforces consistent, robust error handling across all applications within a system. Consistent error handling greatly improves the operations quality and efficiency of an application. Unfortunately, consistent error handling across applications is difficult to attain. The difficulty lies in three areas:

- Not every error condition can be predicted.

- Building the error-handling logic is time-consuming.

- Maintaining consistency of approach is difficult in large projects.

Although Java technology cannot help predict every error condition, it does help address the other two areas. The language's error-handling mechanism allows developers to block off large sections of application code and specify common routines to invoke if an error occurs. Through this approach, the Java virtual machine detects errors and transfers control to the appropriate error routine (see Figure 12.3). This significantly reduces build time and also enforces consis-

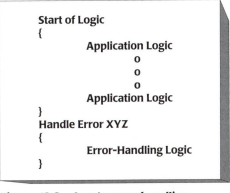

**Figure 12.3   Java's error-handling
approach**

tency through a standardized approach. The Java language does not completely solve the error-handling issue but makes it much easier to handle in a robust, comprehensive manner.

12.4.3 Platform Independence

If an execution architecture has been built for a particular hardware/operating system platform, it is expensive and time-consuming to convert to another platform. This expense makes it difficult to use existing architectures on new projects, even though these architectures may be effective tools. Porting from one platform to another requires architecture changes, may require application changes, and requires thorough retesting of the entire system. Even if a system is written in a standard language such as C, there are differences when porting between platforms.

Java technology was built as a platform-independent language, meaning that a program is written once and then runs on any platform. If an entire execution architecture is written in the Java language, it does not have to be converted. While there have been and continue to be cases of platform-dependent characteristics of Java implementations, especially in the GUI architecture, these issues are relatively minor when compared with C or C++ execution architecture conversion challenges. Java computing's platform independence reduces the need for execution architects to manage platform-dependent functions and lets them borrow more from existing architecture implementations.

Platform independence in execution architectures leads to other efficiencies. Building and using a single architecture even two or three times will save significantly in development cost. Developers can also be trained on a single architecture, and as the developers move from project to project they are knowledgeable about the architecture and programming standards, which results in training cost savings.

12.4.4 Network Communication Building Blocks

Java technology was built with the intention of supporting network-based applications. The Java language supplies routines supporting standard network communications. Time is saved in creating the execution architecture, because these routines can be leveraged and the team does not get involved with the low-level details surrounding network communication.

12.4.5 Security

Security is a major feature of Java technology. Without the security features provided by Java technology, business systems projects would have a tough challenge dealing with security, especially for Internet-based applications. For more information on Java security, see Chapter 15.

12.4.6 Base Classes

The Java language provides useful utility classes for building large business applications. These classes significantly reduce the amount of time required to build fundamental system logic and also provide the entire team with a bug-free set of common routines that are highly reusable.

Even though the Java language has an advantage over other programming languages, some of the common base classes require enhanced functionality to support a business system. Table 12.1 lists examples of where Java's base classes require enhancements.

Table 12.1   Java base class enhancements

Strings
Padding zeros either left or right
Removing spaces
Transposing strings

Dates
Converting strings to/from dates of special formats
Dates outside of the range 1970–2038

12.4.7 Example Solutions on the Web

Developers around the world are solving difficult problems with Java technology and are making their solutions available through the World Wide Web (the Web). As an example, *via* World Network was able to leverage Java classes downloaded from the Web. The project required a framework for a multithreaded Java server to execute business logic. The project used the downloaded code to prove that Java technology was a viable solution for implementing server-side logic. Although this tool was not used in the production version of *via* World Network, it was valuable in building a rapid prototype. A few other solutions found through the Web were purchased and installed in *via* World Network's production system. These solutions reduced the amount of time spent building custom software and improved the operating efficiency of the overall system.

12.4.8 Simpler Object-Oriented Approach

With large projects, the complexity of programming in objects can become difficult to manage. The Java language has simplified object development concepts available in languages such as C++. Java's simpler object syntax assists the project in reducing the challenges associated with object-oriented development. For more information on how the Java language simplifies object development challenges, see Chapter 11.

12.4.9 Third-Party Products Leveraging Java

Interfacing with vendor products constitutes a large portion of an execution architecture. Because Java technology has had such a strong acceptance, software companies are aggressively integrating Java support into their products. Products such as Web servers, database access, and messaging middleware are all incorporating Java technology capabilities. These products are leveraging the advantages of Java technology and are creating solutions tuned to work with Java applications.

12.4.10 Java's Multithreading Capabilities

More and more, business logic is being built to run in application servers that are accessed through the Internet and through intranets. Front-end GUI applications are built to make calls across a network to a centralized processing center. At the processing center, processes are running that service each client request. These programs, to be most efficient and easy to manage, are multithreaded applications that can each handle concurrent client requests. A multithreaded application is one that is able to process simultaneous requests independently.

An example is the process of driving through a toll booth. If there is only one booth, traffic backs up as all drivers pass through the booth sequentially. Alternatively, some toll plazas have multiple booths where drivers simultaneously pay their tolls. This allows multiple cars to pay simultaneously so more traffic can get through the toll plaza in a shorter amount of time. The following example (Figure 12.4) illustrates how a single application performs two functions simultaneously through the use of multiple process threads.

C and C++ multithreaded applications are complicated to write correctly, difficult to test, and a challenge to maintain. Creating a multithreaded application in the Java language is surprisingly simple for programmers familiar with the C and C++ languages. The Java language's easy, safe, and robust multithreaded capabilities assist teams in creating architectures, that support multithreaded applications.

12.5　Java's Shortcomings

It is important to stress that Java technology does not have all the answers. Even though Java technology simplifies and reduces the effort, a significant amount of time is still required to build an execution architecture.

First, even though the Java language provides much of the basic functionality required in an execution architecture, it is not complete. The existing Java classes (Date and String, for example) are not comprehensive enough to cover all of a project's needs. Therefore, the Java classes still must be either wrapped or enhanced by the team building the execution architecture.

Java technology has not solved some of the hardest problems. Teams must still carefully implement multithreading applications despite Java's simplifications. Another example is that technical details of database access must be understood to enable performance tuning of database access.

Another ingredient missing from Java technology is a comprehensive development approach to building the application. Development teams are still required to create standard coding practices, determine the best application framework, train the developers, and ensure consistency across all applications.

12.6　A Java Execution Architecture

To support the implementation of the case studies mentioned in this book, a Java execution architecture was required. A Java execution architecture was initially built for *via* World Network and was used as the starting point for the remaining

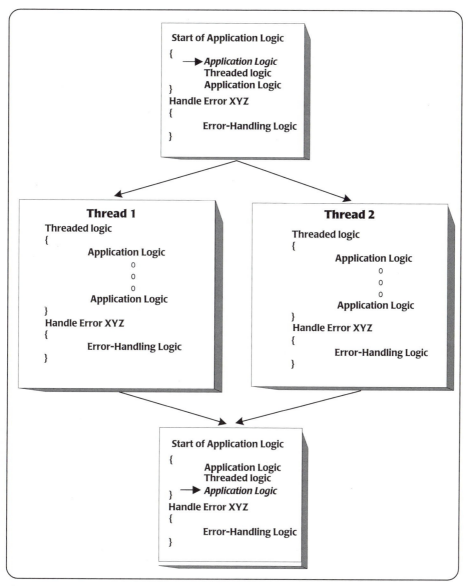

Figure 12.4   Java multithreading

case studies. Through this leverage of the execution architecture, the cost of development was reduced and application development began earlier because programmers did not need to wait for the architecture to be built. The implementation is a full-featured execution architecture supporting multiple types of business applications.

This Java execution architecture supported multiple types of client applications (GUI, voice, kiosk, personal digital assistants, etc.), batch applications, and server-side services. To support all of these functions, 10 percent of the architecture was written in C (Java interfaces are not yet incorporated into all products such as voice response/recognition). Outside of the few C routines, the rest of the architecture was written in Java technology and all applications residing on top of the architecture were written 100 percent in the Java language.

12.6.1 On-line Travel Booking

The on-line travel booking system *via* World Network is described more thoroughly in Chapter 2. Figure 12.5 is a diagram of the execution architecture as it was deployed for *via* World Network. This architecture was designed to provide corporate travelers with multiple methods of accessing common travel management functions. The voice and GUI clients each accessed a common set of pricing, availability, and booking functions that operated as server-side services. A Relational DataBase Management System (RDBMS) managed the traveler's profile and trip information. Batch processing applications maintained the state of pricing and flight information.

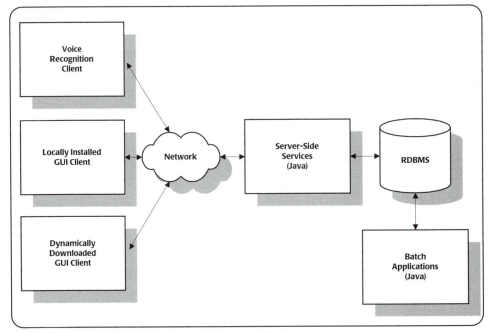

Figure 12.5   *via* **World Network execution architecture**

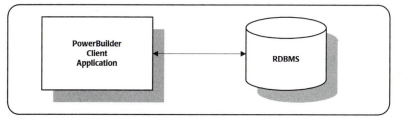

Figure 12.6   Original customer sales support execution architecture

12.6.2 Customer Sales Support System

Another project leveraged the Java architecture to build a working prototype of a Java-based customer sales support system. This prototype is described in more detail in Chapter 3. The system was designed to be used by call centers in supporting customer sales.

This prototype was built as a conversion from an existing client/server system. Figure 12.6 represents the execution architecture of the original system. The Java version of this system (see Figure 12.7) supported dynamic application download, network security, network computer deployment, and cross-platform portability. The prototype also supported the use of new user interfaces leveraging common business logic on the server. The Java implementation of the application took a fraction of the implementation time required for the original system, because converting from PowerBuilder to the Java language was straightforward and the execution architecture from *via* World Network was leveraged.

12.6.3 Call Center Customer Support

The Java architecture was used to implement a system for call center customer support. The new system supported management of documents, such as a customer's bills, and assisted a phone representative in servicing customer calls. It is

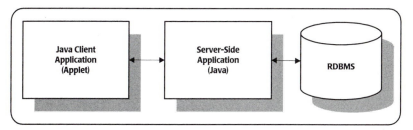

Figure 12.7   New customer sales support execution architecture

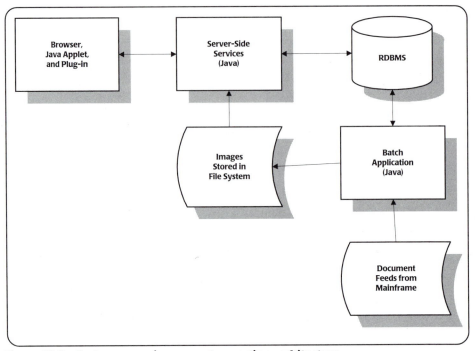

Figure 12.8   Customer service support execution architecture

described in more detail in Chapter 4. The execution architecture for this system is shown in Figure 12.8.

This system was built by tying together a Web browser and Java technology to support the requirements of a call center application. The use of Java technology allowed the system to be easily deployed to all user desktops through their local browser. The implementation leveraged the same Java architecture and integrated third-party products within the browser to supply special image display functions. The Java architecture reduced the implementation time of this system by 50 percent.

12.6.4 Human Resource Service Delivery

The Java architecture built for *via* World Network was used as the starting point for a system designed to virtualize human resource functions (Figure 12.9). Front-end GUI applications were built in JavaScript (with some Java and HTML), and the back-end server-side services were built in the Java language. The prototype application was measured at about 2,000 function points in complexity (approximately 100,000 lines of Java and JavaScript code) and

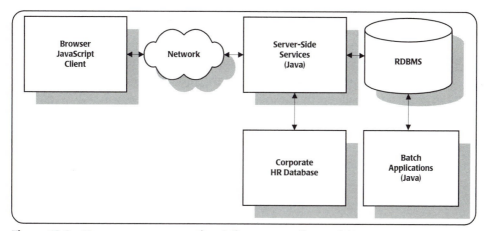

Figure 12.9 Human resource service delivery execution architecture

provided basic human resource functionality to corporate users. The prototype was built in only four months, largely as a result of leveraging an existing Java architecture.

12.7 Summary

Execution architectures are important components of large systems development projects. The examples of business implementations using a Java architecture demonstrate the feasibility of Java technology as a base for building execution architectures that can be leveraged across multiple projects. It is not only feasible but also advantageous to use the Java language, because it provides a number of features that simplify and reduce the cost of building and deploying execution architectures. The savings in time and energy represent dramatic reductions in cost and time to market for new projects. The key messages of this chapter are:

- Companies building large or multiple business systems can benefit by leveraging an execution architecture that addresses common technology requirements.

- Execution architectures simplify and standardize the development of business applications for developers. These architectures can be used across multiple projects.

- The cost and time required to create an execution architecture must be justified by the estimated savings in development and operations costs.

- Java simplifies, enhances, and improves the implementation and operation of execution architectures.

- The use of Java in building an execution architecture faces some challenges (for example, interfaces to third-party products), but the advantages generally outweigh the disadvantages.

CHAPTER THIRTEEN

Moving beyond Applets

13.1   Complex Business Systems

Over the past 30 years, more and more business functions have been automated and enhanced through the use of computing systems. Information technology has become a necessary ingredient in the operation of successful businesses in almost every industry. As the complexity and functionality of these computing systems increase, businesses depend on their availability and performance to a greater and greater extent.

Three examples of complex, mission-critical computing infrastructures for businesses are:

- *Customer billing.* Effective monthly billing of thousands or even millions of customer accounts requires the collection, collation, and pricing of usage records in the utility, financial, and telecommunications industries. Without these systems, companies could not possibly manually bill each customer.

- *Customer support.* Present in nearly all industries are systems that support the immediate retrieval of customer information and processing of customer requests. Customer loyalty has become dependent on the ability of a company's information systems to rapidly and effectively process customer needs.

- *Inventory management and logistics.* Large and small companies track and coordinate the handling/shipping/

processing of customer orders. These systems order materials from suppliers, track inventories in warehouses, and coordinate deliveries of products to customers. Without information systems to manage these complex processes, companies would be less efficient, process fewer orders, and have more customer complaints as a result of late arrivals or lost orders.

Although these are just a few examples of business systems, it is clear that mission-critical information systems are complex and fundamental to the successful operation of companies. This chapter focuses on Java technology and discusses not only its appropriateness for delivering a Web-based front end but also its ability to act as a "server" and provide the core processing for the complex logic of these systems. The idea behind a server is that it performs the complex logic in a centralized location and serves the needs of a large number and wide variety of "clients" or user interfaces. Figure 13.1 illustrates the relationship between clients and servers.

13.2   Implementation Challenges

The focus of this chapter is to identify how the use of Java technology impacts the design, implementation, and operation of the business system. It is not the intent of this chapter to define all of the issues or be a primer regarding the deployment

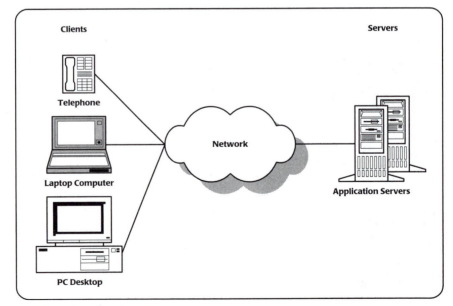

Figure 13.1   Clients and servers

of client/server systems. This chapter focuses on three of the fundamental challenges that are faced by builders of complex Java-based business systems:

- Providing server-side business services

- Successfully deploying client/server applications

- Understanding the impact of emerging standards

13.2.1 Server-Side Business Services

For the business systems described above, the most complex logic in the overall system is not on the client or user interface. The majority of the system's processing logic is on the server. In other words, a company's mission-critical system becomes dependent on the ability successfully to build application servers that process the requests submitted by client applications. Critical issues in the delivery and operation of these servers are as follows.

- *Writing and executing large amounts of application logic.* These systems are the "heart" of complex business systems. Functionality exceeding 10,000 function points (or approximately 500,000 lines of code in a C++ system) is not uncommon for a complex business process.

- *Providing high availability.* Servers generally support multiple users potentially distributed over a wide area. The failure of a server has significantly greater business impact than the failure of a single client.

- *Meeting performance requirements.* Client requests vary over time, and servers must adequately respond to peak load conditions because all requests funnel down to the server. Examples of peak loads include an entire work force all accessing the system at the same time of day and seasonal fluctuations of business volume.

13.2.2 Deploying Client/Server Applications

Distributing application functionality across clients and servers is obviously more complex than centralizing the functionality. The complexity is similar to the challenge faced by a juggler as more balls or plates are added into the mix. Similarly, distributing logic across a network to clients and servers requires more components to be synchronized if the business function is to be performed successfully. Critical concerns in deploying client/server applications are:

- *Providing reliable network connectivity.* By their very nature, clients and servers are distributed. The server must be able to receive and respond to requests that arrive over a network.

- *Securing communications over the Internet.* The use of the Internet to reach both corporate users and customers is rapidly gaining acceptance. The Internet is a public network in which unsecured transmissions can be intercepted and unauthorized requests can be made by third parties. Technologies, tools, and strategies must be deployed to protect confidential data and computing resources.

- *Managing the logical state of a business transaction.* Some complex business processes require multiple interactions between clients and servers, require minutes or even hours of elapsed time to complete, and may involve more than one user interface. How will the state of the logical business transaction be maintained in the case of a server or network failure? How will the logical business transaction state be shared between user interfaces?

13.2.3 Impact of Emerging Standards

ActiveX from Microsoft and the Common Object Request Broker Architecture (CORBA) from the Object Management Group (OMG) are emerging technology standards that provide services to interconnect clients and servers in an object-oriented world. What do these technologies provide and what do they lack? In what ways do these technologies compete? How does a business leverage these services but not lock itself into a technology that eventually loses acceptance and support?

13.3   Java Technology's Role

Java technology can play a pivotal role in improving and simplifying the construction, deployment, and operation of complex client/server business applications. Java technology provides tools and infrastructure that assist in providing server-side business services and in deploying client/server applications.

13.3.1 Providing Server-Side Business Services

Areas where Java provides advantages in developing and deploying server-side business services are as follows.

- *Writing and executing large amounts of application logic.* Developing complex business applications in the Java language is simpler and more efficient than in a language such as C or C++. This is especially true for server-based applications such as *via* World Network, in which significant improvements in application developer productivity were experienced. Refer to Chapters 17 through 20 for more on the impacts of Java technology on developers and application development.

- *Providing high availability.* Java technology can be an integral component in delivering highly available business applications that are able to run day in and day out, 24 hours per day. Chapter 16 explores in detail how Java technology complements existing availability strategies.

- *Meeting performance requirements.* Owing to concerns regarding performance, Java technology's ability to meet the performance requirements of business applications is a key issue. Chapter 14 examines business applications and how Java applications not only can meet performance requirements but also can be advantageous in developing responsive business systems.

13.3.2 Deploying Client/Server Applications

Aspects of deploying client/server applications where Java provides advantages are as follows.

- *Providing reliable network connectivity.* Java base classes simplify and integrate into a single environment the use of Internet-based network protocols. The extensive use of Java technology within the Internet and intranets means that it will continue to be at the forefront of network technology. The base classes and third-party product environment provide a robust environment for reliable network connectivity solutions.

- *Securing communications over the Internet.* Concerns have been raised regarding security issues with Java technology, particularly when it is deployed over the Internet. Chapter 15 explores the concerns regarding Java security for business applications.

- *Managing the logical state of business transactions.* A client application makes a request to a server-side service through the "network" (refer to Figure 13.2). The service performs the request and returns data or status information about the request to the client application.

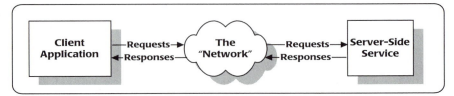

Figure 13.2   Client/server requests and responses

In complex business applications, a request/response series is required to complete a business transaction. Each request is dependent on the business result (a logical state) of the prior transaction. This logical state must be maintained throughout the life of all transactions to complete successfully the overall business transaction. An example is the process for making an on-line purchase:

- Log on and establish authorization to access the system.
- Request product category area X.
- Select product 1.
- Select product 2.
- Request price quote for a combined purchase of both products.
- Confirm purchase.
- Select credit card for purchase.
- Request receipt of purchase to be faxed to office.

There are three approaches to maintaining the logical state of a business transaction during this series of requests/responses:

- Transfer state information with each request/response, which has the disadvantage of resulting in significant delays due to network overhead.
- Maintain an on-line connection between the client and the server-side services throughout the life of the logical business transaction. This approach has significant processing and availability risks for applications that run over the Internet.
- Through the use of a Session Identifier (SID) (see Figure 13.3), transfer a reference to each session with each request/response. The state of the business process is maintained between requests through the SID.

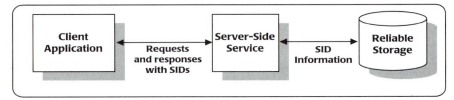

Figure 13.3   Use of a Session Identifier (SID)

The SID is a number that uniquely identifies a business transaction that can be made up of multiple physical requests for service. The first request establishes the SID that is passed with every subsequent request and is available to the server-side services. The network service uses the SID to maintain the state of the overall business transaction across the individual requests. In this way, the information does not have to be transmitted with each request (minimizing network communication time) and the overall system is more reliable because this information is maintained in a highly reliable infrastructure. For more information, refer to Chapter 16, which addresses highly available systems in detail.

13.3.3 Summary of Key Technology Components

The key technology components of a client/server SID infrastructure are as follows (numbers correspond to those used in Figure 13.4).

1. Standards on how a client makes a network service request
2. Tools for converting the network service requests/responses to or from a network compatible request
3. Client application infrastructure to request a SID and to send or receive network service requests

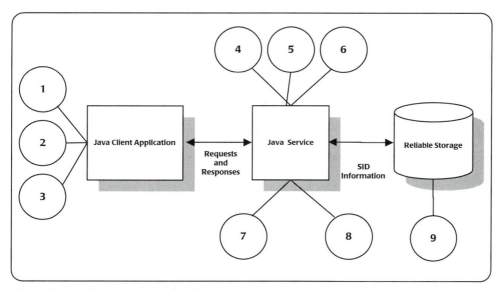

Figure 13.4   Client/server technology components

4. Server-side infrastructure to receive requests, route to the appropriate service, and return responses to the client

5. Server-side infrastructure to create SIDs

6. Server-side infrastructure to make the appropriate SID available to the network service

7. Tools for translating network requests into a form the network service expects

8. Standards for receiving client requests and returning responses and status information

9. Standards/infrastructure for maintaining the state of the overall business transaction

Taking this model one step further (see Figure 13.5), the client interface does not necessarily have to be a Java application. This model was used to build both voice response/recognition (see Chapter 2) and HyperText Markup Language (HTML) (see Chapter 5) user interfaces. Voice response/recognition provided the ability to support users anywhere there is a telephone, whereas HTML is a powerful tool for rapidly creating custom interfaces. In both the voice and HTML user interfaces, technology components 1, 2, and 3 must be created specific to the user interface technology. The good news is that components 4 through 9 are identical for any user interface.

In early 1996, many of the technology components in Figure 13.5 had to be custom developed for building a Java-based business application. Within a year, many of these technology components could be purchased as products or had become part of the Java standard. Significant custom integration is still required, however, because no one vendor provides an end-to-end technology solution that meets all of a complex business system's needs.

13.4   What about ActiveX and CORBA?

There are two key challenges to understanding ActiveX and CORBA when building business systems in Java. The first is that there are competing standards that claim to provide the foundation for building distributed network computing systems. The second challenge is that neither of these competing standards provides the entire infrastructure required to deliver an Internet-based, highly available business system.

Industry analysts and periodicals have for years described the coming age of "distributed network computing." The vision is generally along the lines of a

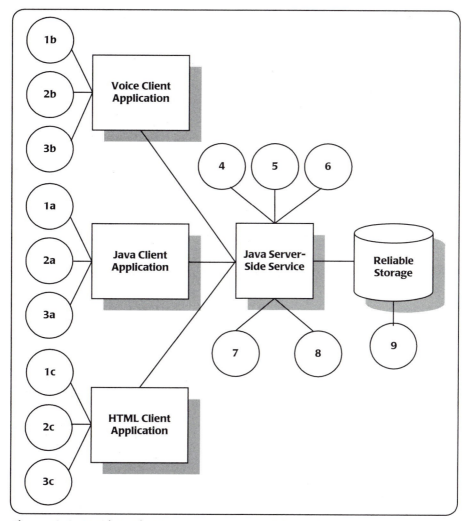

Figure 13.5   Multiple clients access one server-side service

business process object on the "network" that has little or no prior knowledge of who or what may make requests. These requests are received over a network such as the Internet and are successfully processed in a timely, secure, and reliable fashion. The "network" transparently takes care of difficult issues such as security, rollback/recovery from failure, and alternate routing if the network object is busy or down, and makes sure the request takes less than a second to execute. Reality is a long way from this vision, even in a simple, internal company network. The tools, products, and standards are new and in their formative stages and are not yet ready for "prime time."

On the other hand, it is clear that intercommunication between companies has a proven business case as in the example of the emergence of Electronic Data Interchange (EDI) standards. Technologies such as CORBA and ActiveX are attempting to take the EDI concept one step further and provide more powerful tools and infrastructure to perform distributed computing. Instead of having to format messages in a specific format, these tools support the direct interaction between the functionality and the data of remote business objects.

As distributed systems are built, the implementation should either leverage CORBA and/or ActiveX or be prepared to integrate with these technologies. CORBA and ActiveX are to distributed computing what human languages are to communication. These technologies provide the rules and guidelines for how applications work with each other over a network. Like human languages, they also are not compatible and require a translator to communicate. Distributed systems can be built without these technologies, but there should be an expectation that integration with future tools and systems may require CORBA and/or ActiveX. It is best to plan for this eventuality from the start.

13.4.1 Competing Standards

The road is unclear with regard to whether to choose CORBA or ActiveX. Numerous articles and books have been written that expound the merits of each. It is safe to say that these technologies are complex, are difficult to use, and are viewed as competitors. Neither technology has a dominant position as of the late 1990s, yet the competing camps both claim support for the building of Java-based systems.

An emerging solution to the challenge of "which technology do I bet on?" is the use of Java Beans, a standard Java interface for distributed network computing. Whereas Java Beans is closely associated with CORBA, JavaSoft has also provided a bridge (in other words, a translator) to ActiveX. Essentially, the promise of Java Beans is to make the technology choice irrelevant. Although Java Beans is an elegant answer to the dilemma of technology choice, it is also an emerging standard. Emerging standards require time to be adopted and incorporated by third-party software vendors, resulting in an environment with limited numbers of packaged solutions. Business systems developers will have to look closely at the Java Beans technology to determine if it is mature enough to support their requirements.

13.4.2 Real-World Systems

Another challenge that faces the Java business system developer is inherent in the adoption of emerging technologies such as CORBA and ActiveX. Both of these technologies are just beginning to reach a stage of maturity in which complex business systems can be demonstrated, but the infrastructure for integration with existing legacy systems is not in place. Integrations with mainframes, midranges, handhelds, and even voice systems are common requirements in modern business systems. Until either CORBA or ActiveX significantly penetrates this legacy infrastructure, additional third-party products or custom development will be necessary to deploy the business system. Business systems developers should carefully determine the integration requirements for Java-based systems, because manufacturers of products for integration with legacy systems have only recently begun shipping Java versions of their products.

Although the choice of competing standards and the need for integration with existing systems are sufficiently challenging obstacles to building long-lasting and adaptable business systems, additional technological challenges also remain for both CORBA and ActiveX. Distributed network computing technology (both CORBA and ActiveX) emerged out of work for interapplication coordination on the desktop. The challenge in the late 1990s is that distributing this technology over a geographically distributed network is problematic. Issues such as failure/recovery, security over the Internet, scalability, connectivity, and performance become very real and challenging obstacles to distributed object systems. Real-world, commercial systems need to be built today and provide direct business benefits tomorrow, and not be dependent on the eventual emergence of network infrastructure that supports distributed object computing.

So what is a business to do? Essentially, it comes down to the complexity and criticality of the business system being built. If the system is a prototype and a learning exercise, the use and full-scale implementation of technologies such as CORBA, ActiveX. and Java Beans make sense. However, if the Java system is expected to provide demanding performance for critical business systems and to integrate with existing mid-1990s technology, it is the wise business system developer who acknowledges the state of the technology and is prepared to "plug the gaps" in the technology as they are discovered.

13.4.3 An ActiveX–CORBA Survival Strategy

The strategy for supporting CORBA or ActiveX technology may be accomplished through either a custom-developed infrastructure or purchasing of third-party products. In either case, the strategy should focus on two technology components:

- Insulation of server-side services from the specifics of either technology standard

- Tools for translating network requests to a form the network service expects

13.4.3.1 Insulating Server-Side Services

The key to insulating server-side services is to protect the business process from the technology specifics of network communication (see Figure 13.6). The business logic should have no direct tie to the underlying technology and therefore should be able to migrate transparently to the appropriate technology and vendor. As shown in Figure 13.6, the network service is insulated from the underlying server by an additional layer shown as the "insulation layer." The insulation layer is a distinct piece of software with the following functions.

- Translate network communication technologies (for example, CORBA, or ActiveX) formats to a format that the business logic expects.

- Serve as the formal point at which interfaces to external clients are published or made available.

This formal interface not only allows services to work with multiple standards but also is a tool for supporting multiple user interfaces (desktop, voice response, personal digital assistants, etc.).

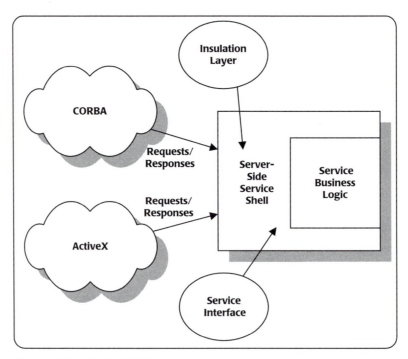

Figure 13.6   Insulation layer

13.4.3.2 Tools for Insulation

Two tools are used to provide the insulation layer and the formal interface definition:

- A shell that enables the business logic developer to define external interfaces

- A tool that generates the translation functions between the business logic and the distributed network computing technology

The shell for the business logic simplifies the development of network computing services for the developer. An analogy of the developer shell can be found in an automobile's automatic transmission. The purpose of an automatic transmission is to make driving a car simpler by relieving the driver of the responsibility of knowing when and how to shift gears. In the same way, the shell for the business logic developer simplifies the building of application services. Through the shell, the business application developer focuses on developing business logic and not on distributed network communication. An added benefit of the shell is enforcement of a consistent approach to building network services. Through this consistent approach to implementing services, a tool is used to translate the interfaces defined by the business application developer into the appropriate network computing technology. As changes in network computing standards or new standards emerge, the tool is appropriately altered but the investment in business logic is preserved.

13.5 Case Studies

All of the case studies (Chapters 2 through 5) are examples of complex business systems that leveraged Java technology. Each of these systems required both client-side and server-side services in order to meet the business requirements.

- **via *World Network*.** The *via* World Network application (Chapter 2) demonstrated Java technology's viability as a client platform, but more importantly demonstrated Java to be a highly effective platform for deploying complex server-side services. More than 15,000 function points of a complex application were built with the Java language to perform travel planning and reservation booking within the server-side services.

- ***Customer sales support.*** This application (Chapter 3) primarily demonstrated Java technology's ability to serve as a complex on-line application platform. This customer sales support application performs complex user interface functionality in an environment that is highly sensitive to long response time.

- *Customer service support.* The implementation for this application (Chapter 4) demonstrated the viability of the third-party product market for Java systems. Java technology provided the glue between a Web browser and a document management utility that ran within the browser. The Java glue customized the solution to meet the customer service support call center's unique requirements.

- *Human resource service delivery.* In this application (Chapter 5), Java technology demonstrated its ability not only to support server-side services but also to integrate with the latest advances in Web server technology and dynamic HTML generation.

13.6   Summary

Building Java-based complex business applications requires careful planning and consideration. Client/server business applications are complex by their very nature, but this difficulty is magnified by current technology trends and the emergence of competing technologies. When building client/server systems with Java technology, it is important to consider:

- The emerging nature of Java technology

- The availability and performance requirements of server-side services

- The reliability, security, and logical state management challenges of deploying Internet-based applications

- The challenges of competing standards for distributed computing (CORBA and ActiveX)

The key considerations in building complex Java-based business systems are as follows.

- Java technology has the capability of providing end-to-end functionality for even the most complex systems. Java technology supports the construction and deployment of complex server-side service applications as well as client-side applications loaded from Web pages.

- Competing distributed computing standards (CORBA and ActiveX) require a well-considered strategy for ensuring that the Java business application does not become dependent on a technology that has lost market interest. Although solutions are emerging within the Java environment, the business system developer should be careful to provide a layer of insulation between the business system logic and unproven, rapidly evolving network computing technologies.

- In most complex business systems, distributed computing technologies (CORBA and ActiveX) does not provide all of the technology answers. The business application development team is required to do some "gap filling" within the technology infrastructure.

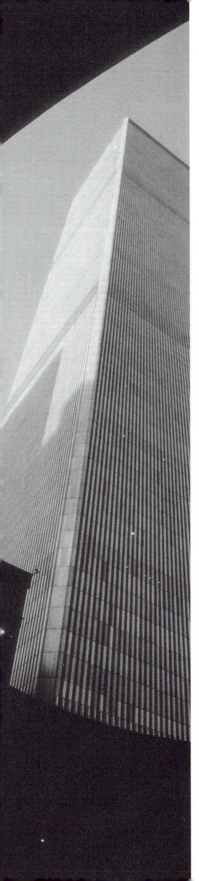

CHAPTER FOURTEEN

Overcoming Performance Challenges

14.1 The Performance of Business Systems

Response time is a critical factor in the success of an application that supports interactive use. Both internal corporate applications and applications that directly support customers must be responsive to maintain efficiency and meet customer service requirements. Examples of internal corporate support applications include:

- Personnel time reporting

- Purchasing and asset management

- Sales support systems

Examples of applications that have stringent performance requirements due to their support of customers include:

- Call-center support systems

- Automated teller machines

- Airline ticketing and reservations

- Internet-based electronic commerce

A customer support/sales call center has demanding performance requirements and serves as a good example of the critical nature of business application performance. In a call center, time is money. The more time spent supporting each customer request, the less efficient the call center. Shorter call time results in more calls taken, more efficient customer service, or more sales per call center agent.

Another industry in which business systems have strict performance requirements is the travel industry. Airline ticketing and reservations systems for the world's largest airlines support tens of thousands of concurrent users and must process thousands of transactions per second. These systems must be very responsive to users, because the product being sold (airline seats) is time sensitive. The customer at the counter does not like to wait and does not accept missing a flight as a result of a slow computer system.

This chapter addresses performance challenges in building business systems with Java technology. It discusses the performance challenges of a new technology, the changes required in business logic, and the changes required in execution architectures to deliver adequate application performance. At the end of this chapter, the performance improvements made in building *via* World Network's Java system are reviewed.

14.2 Challenges of a New Technology

Although Java technology has several quantifiable productivity and quality advantages for building business systems, an area of concern is its ability to meet critical performance requirements. The performance challenges associated with this relatively new application development technology include the following.

- Depending on the functions performed, performance studies after the first full test of *via* World Network's Java-based system showed its performance to be ten to 20 times slower than that of a system based on C or C++.

- Although Java technology has been used extensively as a tool for user interfaces and in working with the Internet, Java technology's use as a platform for developing complex business logic did not emerge until 1997. As a result, relatively little work has been done in tuning Java technology to support complex business logic processing.

- To support platform independence and its security model, Java technology was developed as an interpreted technology. As an interpreted language, each Java statement is evaluated at the time the application is executed. The price of security and platform independence through an interpreted language is a significant performance penalty.

- Application programmers have less experience with Java than with alternative languages and development environments. Having less experience with Java technology may result in less efficient business applications, because application developers do not have enough experience to know how to build highly efficient Java applications.

14.3 Addressing Java Technology Performance

The challenges associated with Java technology performance must be addressed in order to build successful business systems. Although many factors affect performance, those that have the most significant impact to Java applications are:

- *Passage of time.* Java technology's adoption rate is so rapid that strong market demand drives improvements and solutions. These solutions emerge not only in the publicly released version of Java technology but also through third-party products.

- *Improvements in computing power price/performance.* The price/performance of computing continues to improve along the rate predicted by Moore's Law, which predicts the doubling of computer power every 18 to 24 months. These improvements dramatically reduce the cost of providing more power to overcome Java application performance problems.

- *Portability of Java technology.* Building Java applications provides the realistic possibility of choosing the right computing platform at the right time. After the application code for the business system has been written in the Java language, the choice of the computing platform can be made. In contrast, prior business systems development required a decision on the computing platform before the application was built to ensure the application's compatibility with that platform. Waiting until later in the development cycle reduces the risk of choosing a poorly performing hardware platform.

- *High-quality business logic.* The Java language's ability to improve the quality of application code allows development teams the opportunity to switch their focus from resolving bugs to making performance improvements. Many performance problems are firmly rooted within the business logic. When the amount of time spent addressing errors in the business logic is reduced, more time is available to focus on improving the application response time.

- *Predictable and consistent behavior.* Building predictable application logic reduces the challenge of improving performance. Applications behaving with consistent characteristics can be improved through broad, overall solutions.

• *Scalable business logic design.* Platforms and technologies continuously improve; however, the business logic is often the most difficult to change and the most likely to be a bottleneck. Through the design of applications that anticipate bottlenecks and implement strategies to provide for scalable growth, business systems can be built that will provide consistent performance as use increases.

14.4 *via* World Network–Java Performance

In 1996, *via* World Network developed a large-scale complex business system in Java. Through the second half of 1996 and the first half of 1997, dramatic improvements in Java performance were leveraged by *via* World Network to create a production-quality system. The areas that had the greatest impact on performance were:

• Passage of time

• Improvements in price/performance

• Portability of Java

• High-quality business logic

• Predictable and consistent behavior

• Scalable business logic design

14.4.1 Passage of Time

During the development of the *via* World Network system, a strong and competitive environment for Java high-performance solutions emerged, including just-in-time (JIT) compilers, which convert Java applications into native machine instructions rather than interpreting each instruction. Interpreted code is a generic language that allows Java applications to be platform independent, but with interpreted code and platform independence comes a performance penalty. JIT compilers offset this problem by converting the interpreted instructions into the native machine language at runtime. A JIT compiler enables the Java application to run significantly faster and in some cases results in a tenfold improvement in performance.

In addition, the basic Java Development Kit (JDK) underwent significant improvements. The JDK is the basic version of Java that can be downloaded from the JavaSoft Web site. Although the JDK uses an interpreter and is slower than a

JIT compiler, the improvements in the JDK implementation increased the speed of application development as developers were able to test applications faster.

Creating efficient compilers is a dynamic field in which vendors leapfrog each other's implementations on a consistent basis. This competitive environment drives continued improvement in the performance of Java technology. Through the use of JIT compilers, the determining factor of price/performance becomes the overall performance of the platform.

14.4.2 Improvements in Price/Performance

Computing power continues to grow by leaps and bounds. During 1996 alone, the computing power of the major vendors of personal computers and data center servers more than doubled while the relative price remained constant. New models of processors emerged (Pentium II and UltraSPARC, for example), and the clock speeds of these and existing processors continue to increase.

One of the most important improvements, although possibly the least noticed, was the dramatic decrease in the cost of memory over the course of 1996. Memory is critical for application performance, especially for applications that perform services on behalf of clients. The more memory in a machine, the more likely the application will stay resident in memory as it executes and not have to store data or parts of the program on disk. Reduced memory costs help business application developers ensure that applications consistently reside in memory.

The price/performance of client/server platforms has reached a stage in which processing power is inexpensive. The improvement has become so great that most on-line business transactions can be serviced in less than 1 second even when written in the Java language. The focus should be on identifying business logic that is exceptional in either volume or processing requirements. With the focus on improvements in this exceptional logic, processing power handled the response time requirements of the majority of the *via* World Network system's business logic.

14.4.3 Portability of Java

In the past, performance benchmarks were performed early in the development of a business system because of the impact a platform had on the actual code being developed. Using Java technology, the business logic can now be developed on one platform and then its performance on that platform can be compared with its performance on other platforms at the end of the development cycle. Moving hundreds of thousands of lines of Java code from one platform to another becomes an exercise in organization and software control, because software conversion is not required.

With *via* World Network, the application was successfully ported to a second server platform in order to leverage a lower-processing-cost platform. The lesson learned was to make an initial decision on processing platform based on the best information available, but not go through rigorous performance benchmarking of platforms early in the development cycle. As part of the system and volume test exercise, the application should be tested on multiple platforms and the results of these tests then used to drive the growth in equipment to meet the volume requirements of the business.

The choice of one platform over another is often based on comparative industry performance benchmarks that measure the time taken to process mathematical and business transactions. The challenge is in determining how these benchmarks relate to the business requirements of the moment. The good news is that Java technology's platform independence helps to solve this problem. In the past, platform decisions had to be made before the business logic was created, because of the requirement of building to a platform's unique specifications. By building platform-independent applications, the platform decision can be made after some or all of the business logic has been written. More accurate data leads to better, just-in-time platform decisions.

14.4.4 High-Quality Business Logic

Investments in improving the quality of the business logic paid off immediately during the system and volume testing of the *via* World Network application. Although the project might have saved one to two weeks in delivery time and might have saved roughly 1 percent of the development effort by not putting the emphasis on quality reviews during development, this time was easily made up during a two month system test. During the first week of system testing, the team was focused primarily on performance improvements instead of on bugs and defects in the implementation of a large, complex system.

The development of higher-quality applications through quality checks and reviews is a big part of ensuring the timely and on-budget delivery of business systems. Although this concept is not specific to Java programming, the Java language promotes development of higher-quality applications than those promoted by C or C++. Through simpler syntax, improved memory management, and solid error-handling features, Java applications are easier to build, easier to review, and of higher quality than C and C++ implementations. This allows the project team to focus on performance rather than tracking down application bugs.

14.4.5 Predictable and Consistent Behavior

Applications in a business system should be developed within common frameworks (or shells), and complex technology functions (such as network communications and database access) should be accessed through simple interfaces. The approach of using frameworks and standard interfaces insulated *via* World Network's business application developers from the technology and ensured consistent implementation of all business logic. The intent was to:

- Simplify development.

- Focus the developers on business logic, not technology details.

- Minimize the long-term operational cost of the business application.

Through the use of frameworks and standard interfaces, technology experts were able to address database and Java application performance issues on a systemwide basis instead of on an application-by-application basis. For example, improvements in database access logic and underlying Java implementation were made easier through this layering strategy. The business would neither have had the time nor been able to afford the cost of making these types of technology changes on a one-by-one basis with hundreds of unique implementations.

14.4.6 Scalable Business Logic Design

Although scalable business logic design is not an area specific to Java systems, certain concepts must be considered when building a high-volume business system regardless of which technology is used. There are three primary areas of focus in building scalable business systems.

- Provide infrastructure for transparent distribution of system processing

- Provide for processing scalability

- Provide for database scalability

Support for scalable system execution and operation is a concept that must be present from the beginning of the development cycle. Essentially, business application developers should not make assumptions on where their applications run and where requests are serviced. An insulating layer should be present to allow applications and service providers to be transparently distributed. As a matter of practice, it is better not to distribute application processing unless performance or existing system requirements dictate this solution. Why add the complexity of distributed processing if it is not needed? In those cases where it is needed, it is much easier to adapt to these challenges if the insulation is in place.

Application processing should be scalable. The focus is to identify bottlenecks where application behavior overwhelms existing processing power. An example of this was seen in *via* World Network's ticket pricing function. Eventually, as the *via* World Network system increased in volume, the processing of the pricing function had to be increased to keep pace with demand. If, in this case, the pricing function had not been scalable, the solution would have been to scale the processing platform (an expensive alternative that would have had its limits). An alternative strategy was taken that was less expensive and easier to scale by having the *via* World Network application transparently access one of many pricing functions executing on multiple processing servers. In this way, the pricing function leveraged lower-cost equipment and was scaled faster, because it was easier and faster to add low-cost servers rather than to make expensive platform upgrades.

Database scalability is another frequent bottleneck of business applications. It is critical that the applications not be dependent on the physical location of the database resource, because database resources are best scaled through the addition of more platforms. Hiding the physical access of the database from the business application allows the system to grow its database resource in a cost-effective manner while hiding the addition of the new platform from the business logic. In the *via* World Network example, the access of the master reservation database was insulated from the application developer. At runtime, the database request was routed to the appropriate physical server, enabling the *via* World Network system to scale its database processing needs easily. Additional database server processing could be added without having to change any of the *via* World Network business application logic.

14.5   *via* World Network Business Logic

During stress testing and performance tuning exercises, several areas in which the Java-based *via* World Network system could be improved were discovered. Although many of the improvements that were made can be applied to business systems written in any language, they are also important considerations for a Java-based system. The following are areas where the most significant application-level performance gains were achieved in the *via* World Network system.

- In-memory table loads

- Message logging

- Global object declaration

- Redundant object instantiation

- Object creation and control structures

14.5.1 In-Memory Table Loads

Many business systems require on-line, real-time analysis and lookups. For data that remains relatively static (changes no more than once per day for example), the data can be loaded into memory to reduce the overhead associated with network access of database resources. Good candidates for in-memory loads include: code/decode lookups, industry rules, and internal reference data. In the *via* World Network system, significant improvements in application performance were achieved by loading static industry fare information into memory.

14.5.2 Message Logging

As part of the infrastructure supporting the *via* World Network business application, logging facilities were developed. These message logging facilities supported *via* World Network's developers in providing runtime data about application processing in the areas of debugging, warnings, fatal errors, and performance information. Although message logging was critical for successful *via* World Network operations, it can lead to problems if overused. This is especially important in Java applications, where excessive object creation leads to problems with the performance of the memory management functions. It is important to have the ability to turn logging off during normal operation and to review application code to ensure that the developers have not excessively logged information.

14.5.3 Global Object Declaration

Data storage for runtime objects was carefully reviewed in the *via* World Network application. To conserve memory space, it is important that objects be declared and used in the same localized area. Too often, variables are declared globally across the entire application, leading to a considerable waste in memory space. This becomes especially important in Java applications, because the overhead of Java memory management can be significant. The more objects that the Java virtual machine has to keep track of, the greater the performance impact of memory management.

14.5.4 Redundant Object Instantiation

Instantiating (or creating) an object essentially means creating memory space for the object. In a Java program it is important to look for cases where an object is instantiated within one part of the application and returned to a calling application. If the calling application also instantiates this object, the returned object is essentially copied back to the calling application. The result is time-consuming because Java's memory management functions create two copies of the same object and the data is copied from one object to the other for no benefit.

14.5.5 Object Creation and Control Structures

If an object is going to be used only within a programming control structure (such as if/then, while loop, etc.), the object should be declared in the structure and not outside of it. Declaring the object outside the structure requires the memory management routines to create the object even if the control structure condition logic dictates that the logic will not be executed.

14.6 *via* World Network Execution Architecture

An execution architecture implements the technology underneath the business logic. It contains the technically complex code that simplifies the business application's interface to the underlying technical implementation (for example, network communication or database access). For more on execution architectures, see Chapter 12. Following is a list of areas in which improvements were made in the *via* World Network execution architecture. These example improvements will help other Java-based business systems avoid similar problems.

- In-memory table storage size

- Java String and Date objects

- Memory heap size of the Java interpreter

- Database access

- Message logging

14.6.1 In-Memory Table Storage Size

The initial implementation of in-memory database table loads quickly became a memory storage problem. Database data that took 1 megabyte to store on disk was taking more than 40 megabytes to store in memory. This size expansion occurred because a new Java object was created for each element in each row of data loaded. The application quickly ran out of memory space and overall execution also slowed down as memory management facilities were overtaxed.

Two solutions were developed. The first solution was to force the Java virtual machine's memory management routines to execute during the initial loading of the data. This allowed the virtual machine to clean up memory as it was being released and brought the relative size of data storage down by ten times (for example, 10 megabytes in memory reduced to 1 megabyte). The second strategy was a combination of tactics that compressed the size of the application data. Fewer objects were created, Java Integers rather than Java Date objects were stored, and redundant data fields were eliminated through the use of pointers. In some cases, this compression strategy reduced the footprint from 1 megabyte to 100 kilobytes of memory space.

14.6.2 Java String and Date Objects

In business applications, string and date objects are called frequently by developers. To ensure consistent use and to provide a way to make future improvements, all of the native Java String and Date objects were wrapped by a layer of custom software created by the *via* World Network project team. By having the application logic insulated from the native Java implementation of String and Date, improvements were implemented in only one place and not throughout the entire application. Through custom improvements and the purchase of third-party product software, significant improvements in the storage and performance of string and date objects were made. These improvements resulted in performance gains of more than ten percent for the application.

14.6.3 Memory Heap Size of the Java Interpreter

Because of the size of the application and the amount of data being loaded into memory, the application ran into constraints on the amount of memory the Java virtual machine could use for processing. The heap is the area of memory used by the virtual machine for storing and managing application variables; the default heap size is 1 megabyte. By increasing the size of the heap area to 40 megabytes, overall runtime improvements of 25 percent were achieved. Even greater improvements (over 99 percent) were seen during the start-up of the application when database tables were loaded into memory.

14.6.4 Database Access

A critical factor in developing high-performance applications is reduction of the amount of time Java applications spend accessing database resources. To fulfill its performance requirements, *via* World Network was forced to use the most sophisticated database access logic available from a database vendor. This logic was written in the C language and forced the team to use the Java native method call interface. *via* World Network was required to spend significantly more than the planned amounts of time and energy in developing and tuning this interface.

14.6.5 Message Logging

The ability to turn message logging on and off is a powerful feature, but it can be a performance bottleneck. Such a bottleneck occurred in complex *via* World Network application processing in which layers of software components call other layers of components. As the call depth grows, each new component must be checked to determine the appropriate logging level. The overhead of checking logging levels becomes a major performance penalty when three or more levels of components are called to service a request. It is important in this case to support a global logging level that can apply to all components and reduce the amount of time spent in checking levels and creating objects.

14.7   *via* World Network Results

To measure a Java application's ability to perform complex, real-world business transaction processing, one should compare an all-Java solution with an existing industry solution. One example is in the area of airline ticketing and booking, specifically the pricing of tickets. As a result of the complexities of fares and rules regarding ticket pricing, a significant amount of processing is required to price a ticket at the lowest possible fare. Pricing a ticket involves scanning tremendous amounts of reference data as well as constructing multiple forms of the ticket (one-ways, round trips, etc.) to ensure the lowest possible fare for the customer. To price a four-coupon, coach class U.S. domestic ticket, the typical response time from mainframe-based reservation systems in the mid-1990s was from two to five seconds.

via World Network's pricing system was required to have the same performance characteristics as existing mainframe-based reservation systems. Through application of the techniques documented in this chapter over a five-month period, the time required for pricing of tickets through the *via* World Network Java system was reduced from 90 minutes to a level on a par with that of mainframe-based systems. Moreover, this pricing functionality was performed on low-cost client/server computing platforms. Scaling this Java-based pricing system was as simple as adding another server.

The performance improvements outlined above were made in the *via* World Network application from mid-1996 to mid-1997. Figure 14.1 shows the impact of the improvements on pricing performance. In only five months, the processing time for pricing a four-coupon coach class ticket was reduced from 15 minutes to approximately 10 seconds between August 1996 and January 1997.

14.8 Summary

Java technology suffers from performance challenges, but high-volume, high-performance Java systems have been built with the response times of existing world-class business systems. Although specific application and execution architecture enhancements have been made (and have been documented here), the key to success has been in implementing a performance strategy. In approaching the challenge of performance, it is important to remember the following facts.

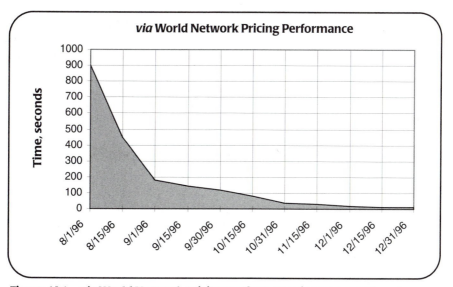

Figure 14.1 *via* **World Network pricing performance improvement**

- As companies rely more and more on computer systems, performance becomes an increasingly important challenge and is sometimes the key to the success of the system.

- Java application development must consider the performance challenges associated with the use of Java technology.

- Over time, Java technology has matured and its performance has rapidly improved.

- Java technology's adoption rate is so strong that the market continues rapidly to develop performance tools and Java language improvements.

- The continuing acceleration in computing platform price/performance improvements helps to reduce the challenge of developing high-performance Java applications.

- The portability of Java applications enables businesses to make platform decisions later in the development cycle, thereby better ensuring the adoption of the right platform at the right time.

- Building high-quality business logic is a critical determinant of success. Inefficient code can be written in any language, and the time spent fixing and debugging is time lost in making performance improvements.

- Predictable and consistent behavior is a critical ingredient of holistic performance improvements across large business systems. Without a consistent implementation, improvements are made only at focused points in the application, which reduces the overall impact on any one performance improvement.

- Just as any system in any language can be written poorly, any programming language can build business logic that is not scalable and that causes bottlenecks at critical application points. Three key areas of focus should be carefully addressed to minimize application bottlenecks: transparent distribution of application processing, processing scalability, and database scalability.

- Application logic should be closely reviewed to ensure that the logic is efficiently designed and implemented. In several areas (object declaration and control structures, for example), simple techniques can eliminate inefficient processing.

• Improvements in the business system's execution architecture can have significant impacts on overall system performance. The use of memory, date, and string objects and the access of database resources are example areas in which improvements to the execution architecture can have significant impacts on performance.

CHAPTER FIFTEEN

Making Applications Secure

15.1　Internet Security for Businesses

Using the Internet as a tool for low-cost and widespread access to customers and/or employees has rapidly gained popularity. Use of the Internet for business transactions comes with security risks, however. What gives the Internet its widespread reach is also what gives it its greatest security weakness: simple and easy access to a public network. Although simple access makes the Internet a powerful tool for business, it is also easy for unauthorized people to view and attack Internet-based applications.

There are several areas of concern regarding use of the Internet for business systems. Businesses must be careful to ensure that sensitive customer and corporate data is secured as it is transmitted over the Internet. Another area of concern is the exposure of the company to malicious attacks by means of the Internet. Finally, the business has to ensure that the system put in place does not increase the danger of malicious attack of customer or employee desktops.

This chapter focuses on the security issues related to development of Java applications that run over the Internet. Specifically, this chapter deals with concerns that have been raised about the use of Internet-based Java applications. These concerns should be considered, but they should not be reason for rejecting Java technology as a tool for delivering applications over the Internet. This chapter discusses the reasons why Java technology is viable for Internet-based applications and also considers the areas in which businesses should focus their security considerations.

15.2   Security Concerns of Java

Owing to the ability of Java applications to be dynamically downloaded over the Internet, concerns have been raised about the possibility of malicious Java applications attacking the computers of unsuspecting users. Three of the most important security risk scenarios are as follows.

- A user accesses a Web page and unsuspectingly downloads a Java application that infects the user's computer with a virus or perpetrates some other malicious act such as deleting files or stealing passwords.

- A Java application inappropriately accesses data on a user's hard drive or within a corporate network.

- A hacker intercepts the user's request and inserts a malicious application in place of the one the user believes is being downloaded.

The original developers of Java recognized these risks and challenges and developed checks and controls to address them. Two of Java's most important controls are:

- Evaluating every Java command at execution time to ensure that the application is not accessing areas of the computer's memory or performing commands that are not appropriate

- Working with vendors of browser technology to ensure that Java applications that are downloaded over the Internet are not allowed to access protected areas of hard disk

Despite this work, holes in the Java implementation have been found by researchers and have received significant publicity. These holes were valid issues and concerns that needed to be addressed. Both JavaSoft and the browser vendors have responded quickly to these concerns to minimize the potential for malicious activity.

15.3 | Reasons Not to Worry

The holes discovered in the Java implementations are significant and require effort to address, and additional holes in the implementation of Java technology may also be discovered. However, this is not a reason to reject the use of Java technology for business applications, because there are several reasons why the concern over security has been overstated.

- Breaking Java has become a "sport."

- Before Java, downloaded application security was not a problem.

- Java applications can be installed locally.

15.3.1 Breaking Java Has Become a "Sport"

Although it is strange to say it is good that something is being broken, this is the case for Java technology. The people who are making the announcements about security holes in Java implementations are academic researchers intent on improving the technology. These researchers are discovering the flaws and are publishing their results so that Java implementers can make the appropriate fixes. In effect, Java technology has an Internet-based quality assurance team that is trying to find the flaws and problems before they are discovered by hackers. Any technology can be broken and taken advantage of, and Java technology is fortunate in having an aggressive community that is intent on improving its security.

15.3.2 Before Java, This Was Not a Problem

Before the advent of Java technology, dynamically downloaded applications were unheard of. Although the technology of downloading at runtime is not revolutionary, the ability to do this over the Internet and to follow a security model is revolutionary. C, C++, and popular development packages do not have this capability. The holes discovered in the Java security model are not permanently damaging and have generally been fixed by application of patches. The security risk of Java technology is much lower than that of the millions of Internet users who regularly download applications from the Internet and install them on their local machines. These applications range in functionality from news readers to Internet browsers to multimedia display tools. Generally, these applications have no runtime security and could easily install a virus or cause havoc in a local machine or corporate intranet.

15.3.3 Java Applications Can Be Installed Locally

Just as standard desktop applications can, Java applications can be run from a local hard drive instead of being dynamically downloaded. If corporate standards forbid dynamic downloading or installation of applications downloaded from the Internet, a Java application can be rolled out to users in the same manner that a word processing or spreadsheet package is installed. In this manner, desktop support personnel can provide the ultimate assurance that applications (including those written in the Java language) are properly installed and are from approved sources.

Java applications are based on a technology more secure than alternative application development technologies. Figure 15.1 depicts the additional security Java computing provides, which is where the security concerns are being raised. Security issues are a concern because Java technology attempts to address these challenges. If the company or customers continue to distrust its security, Java technology can be used in a manner similar to that of existing technologies. By installing Java locally on an end-user's computer, the application will continue to execute successfully as if it were a C or C++ program.

15.4 Developing Secure Applications

Assuming that the platform is secure and will not violate the integrity of a user's computer, businesses should be more concerned about the following security issues.

- Communicating in a manner that is "Internet-friendly"

- Reliably and securely transmitting information over the Internet

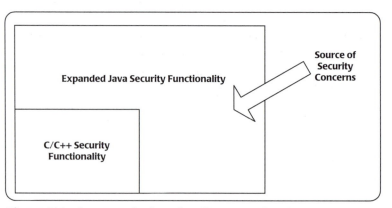

Figure 15.1   Java security functionality versus C or C++

These concerns are focused on delivering complex business systems that are not simple Java applications accessing back-end Web servers. Generally, a complex business system has logic or application code with runs at a data center somewhere in the Internet. This logic, which is "in the network," is the core of the business application and performs the essential logic that delivers the business function. In the cases of booking travel arrangements or performing human resource services, the logic that runs in the network is the reservation and pricing engine. This logic is complex and is significantly beyond the capability of a Web server to support. In these examples, the user's Java application must communicate with a back-end application engine through the Internet. This communication must be secure and also must easily integrate into existing corporate Internet implementations (or in other words, be "Internet-friendly").

15.4.1 "Internet-Friendly" Communications

The key here is to roll out applications to Internet users rapidly and to work seamlessly within a corporate Internet implementation. Corporate Internet connections are generally secured by a firewall that prevents unauthorized or potentially dangerous communications over the Internet. TCP/IP is a basic form of most client/server communications, but is considered open, dangerous, and prone to attacks by Internet hackers. Owing to the danger of allowing TCP/IP communications to or from the Internet, very few corporations allow this form of communication to pass across their firewalls.

An alternative to using the basic tools provided with TCP/IP is to use the communication protocol of the Web. This protocol is known as HyperText Transfer Protocol (HTTP) and is the basis for all Internet browser communications to Web servers on the Internet. HTTP is actually based on TCP/IP but adds additional functionality for its use on the Internet. Most corporations allow communication with the Internet to take place as long as it uses this protocol. Essentially, HTTP has become the de facto standard for secure client/server communications over the Internet. As part of its standard release, Java provides simple tools for communicating through HTTP to or from a Java application.

15.4.2 Reliable and Secure Transmissions

HTTP will pass through corporate firewalls, but the information being passed can easily be read by probing eyes. For secure communication of information such as credit card numbers, the information within the HTTP message must be encrypted. Browsers implement a secure form of HTTP by using a technology known as Secure Socket Layer (SSL). This technology allows a browser to communicate securely with a Web site that supports secure communications.

The challenge for building secure, Internet-friendly business systems is in leveraging both HTTP and SSL to communicate over the Internet between a Java client application and network-based business processes (see Figure 15.2). The Java client application leverages the browser and the Web server's ability to communicate securely in an Internet-friendly manner using HTTP and SSL. The Web server is modified to capture requests from the client and to pass them to the business logic processing the request.

15.5   Summary

Concerns over the security of Java applications have been overstated and have lost sight of the bigger picture. Security of business applications leveraging the Internet is improved by the Java security model and its ability to work easily with existing Web browser, Internet communication, and security protocols. Businesses should focus on how these technologies are leveraged to deliver Internet-based business processes that communicate in a secure and Internet-friendly manner. The primary considerations in using Java to build Internet-based applications are as follows.

- Security has always been an important requirement of business systems, but building applications that run over the public Internet adds challenges and complexity to that requirement.

- Since Java technology was released, concerns have been raised about the robustness of its security model.

- Java technology provides additional security functionality beyond what is provided by C or C++ environments. It is in this additional functionality that security problems are being discovered.

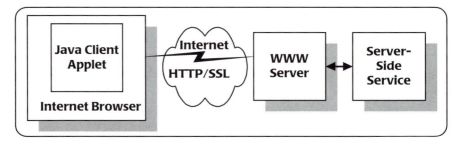

Figure 15.2   Secure Internet communications

- Security issues with Java technology are being closely watched and examined. The significant community of interest surrounding Java technology helps to ensure that the problems that exist are discovered and resolved quickly.

- Java applications do not have to be dynamically downloaded. It is through this form of downloading that many of the concerns regarding Java technology are raised. When a Java application is installed on a user's machine, it behaves the same as if it were a locally installed C or C++ application.

- Successful Internet applications that communicate to corporate customers must consider the security concerns of the corporation. Most corporations will allow only HTTP for communications through their corporate firewalls.

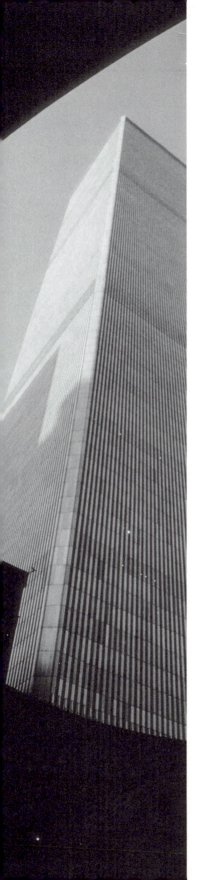

CHAPTER SIXTEEN

Building Highly Available Systems

16.1 Business System Requirements

An example of a business system that must provide highly available transaction processing services is *via* World Network's flight reservations facility for business travelers. Corporate customers' travel arrangements change frequently, and often these customers make travel arrangements at odd hours of the night or weekend. For example, a business traveler arrives at a hotel late in the evening and checks his or her corporate voice or e-mail, only to discover that he or she is not traveling to Detroit the next day but instead must go to Chicago. This traveler will not have time during the day or at the airport to change reservations and must make travel arrangements immediately. If the reservation system is unavailable or not responding, the customer will lose confidence in the service. Multiplied by many such experiences, adoption by the market will be slow, at best.

Another example of a business system that requires high availability requirements is the customer call center support system. In a system built to support customer bill queries, the appropriate bill must be retrieved and reviewed by the support agent during the first few seconds of the customer's phone call. If the customer has to wait or call back later when the system is available, the potential for losing the customer increases. In the same way, a customer sales support system must be available if the business is to capture a customer's order. Customers will call the competition's call center if they have to wait or call back later.

Java technology can be used to deliver business systems that have a higher degree of availability than comparable systems built in C or C++. This is not to say that Java technology is the complete answer to building a highly available business system, but Java provides significant advantages over traditional client/server application environments.

16.2 Implementation Challenges

Modern business systems are challenged by the complexity, lack of control, and relative "newness" of Internet-based services and also by the significant challenge of highly reliable operations on client/server platforms. These systems have more components and less reliability than comparable mainframe implementations. Through the operation of multiple client/server systems for more than ten years, a valuable lesson has been learned: *everything can and will fail.* Client/server disk drives, application processing, network connectivity, processing platforms, and database technology are not as dependable as their mainframe counterparts. In general, the best strategy is to avoid single points of failure through redundant implementation of components. Disk drives and the data they store can be mirrored, redundant processing platforms and network communications facilities can be installed, and parallel server strategies for highly reliable databases can be implemented. However, none of these strategies deals with the single most important area in the building of a network service system—application processing logic reliability and availability.

The application processing logic is the heart of the system. The logic is what performs the business process and makes the whole event meaningful. It is crucial that this logic be available for each transaction sent by a user. Client/server systems have a tremendous challenge in the availability of the business logic because of the language and environment in which they are primarily written, C or C++. These languages are the most common and appropriate languages for client/server platforms. Unfortunately, these languages were built more for technical programmers and not for business application developers. These languages require sophisticated understanding of application memory management and error handling to develop highly available applications. Improper memory handling results in memory "leaks." As memory leaks, the application uses more and more system memory with each transaction. Eventually, the platform runs out of memory and the application fails. Generally, business application developers do not handle memory well and leaks are common—not an auspicious beginning for systems that are to be available all the time and that will be compared with 20- to 30-year-old systems that already have most of their bugs ironed out.

Error handling in either C or C++ is also a challenge for business developers. Error handling is, by its very nature, a complex undertaking and is often improperly or ineffectively implemented by nontechnical business application developers. Proper handling of and transparent recovery from a system error so that the user is unaware of it are difficult for even a sophisticated technical developer. Harder still are understanding the root cause of an error and retracing the path that a transaction took through application logic. In traditional mainframe environments, traces of an application's logic path at the time the system produced an error are available. On client/server C or C++ platforms, trapping and tracing the paths of application and system errors are very difficult and rarely performed.

The first step in building a highly available business system is to select the platform strategy. Should the system rely on a vendor that specializes in highly available computing, or should a multivendor strategy be taken? The second step in building a highly available system is using Java technology to address challenges in the area of application resilience.

16.2.1 Single-Vendor Strategies

There are several companies that offer excellent products for implementing highly available systems. (Two of the most successful are Stratus and Tandem.) Although these companies have different technical strategies, the business strategies of their highly available products are the same: deliver highly available systems through hardware and system software that are redundant in nature. These systems offer many attractions, not the least of which is their presence in the airline, telecommunications, and financial services industries, in which they perform data communications and transaction processing. A single-vendor strategy also simplifies the navigation through a complex environment of technological choices. Unfortunately, highly available business systems often are not built on these platforms for the following reasons.

- *Price/performance.* Although these vendors demonstrate comparable price/performance to industry leaders in client/server platforms, this is accomplished through sophisticated tuning and preparation of their products. In addition, these products generally are expanded in large, expensive increments. A responsive business system requires a more dynamic platform that scales inexpensively as transaction volume increases. Surges in system usage require rapid responses to continuously meet user performance and availability expectations. Incremental upgrades in the highly available system environments could take six months or more of intense planning and preparation.

- *Industry standards and third-party product support.* The highly available processing platforms lack widespread third-party product support for both hardware and software. Because of the specialized nature of these platforms, third-party vendor support is sparse and the companies themselves have been slower that general purpose competitors in keeping up with the latest advances in network computing technology (such as Web protocols, Internet firewall technology, and local area network communications) and business application development (for example, graphical software development tools and object-oriented languages).

- *Application resilience.* Single-vendor platforms typically present just as many challenges as multivendor environments, and sometimes more. C and C++ are the languages used in single-vendor environments; however, the highly available systems require the use of special software to enable the application logic to be highly available as well. Special software for highly available computing is technical in nature and poses a challenge for business process developers. In the end, the business application developer is left with the same C and C++ challenges as well as the additional burden of learning and adapting to the unique environments of these highly available systems. This additional burden translates into longer system development cycles, which often are not acceptable because of the nature of the business environment.

16.2.2 A Multivendor Strategy

Through the use of multiple client/server vendors that do not specialize only in high-availability computing, a reliable and cost-effective business system can be built. Enabling this strategy was the rapid improvement in the early 1990s of products by these vendors that delivered low-cost, highly available platforms relying on the use of redundant hardware. An example of this environment is illustrated in Figure 16.1.

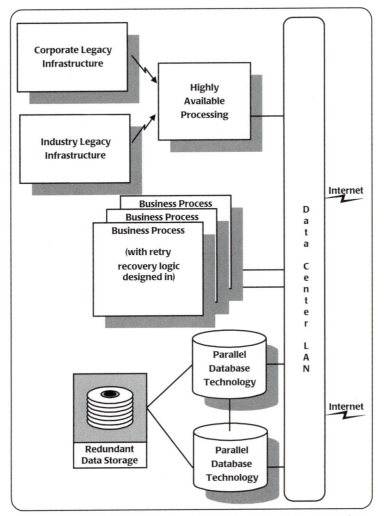

Figure 16.1   Multivendor strategy for highly available computing

This strategy depends on a number of hardware and software systems to deliver highly available computing. The key is to eliminate single points of failure through redundancy. Key redundant components include:

- *Network connections.* There are two connections to all external networks. Generally, network devices are intelligent enough to reroute requests to the available connection automatically.

- *Parallel database technology.* Through the use of two servers that constantly monitor each other and have access to the same storage, highly available database technology is a reality.

- *Redundant data storage.* By leveraging the low-cost disk drives in redundant configurations, highly available data storage is achieved cost effectively.

- *Processing servers.* Redundant application logic residing on multiple servers is also a critical component of highly available applications. It is critical that the processing be independent between the servers to minimize complex interdependencies. If the servers depend on each other, they are dependent rather than redundant. A failure in one will cause a failure in the other.

Hardware and system software redundancy alone will not solve the challenge of building a highly available, Internet-based client/server system. In fact, hardware redundancy is the easy part of the solution. The real challenges are to:

- Recover reliably from failures without the user realizing that there was a problem.

- Reduce application logic defects that result in downtime.

- Allow for rapid identification and resolution of application logic errors.

16.3   The Role of Java Technology

Although Java technology does not provide tools for improving the reliability of client/server disk drives, processing platforms, and networks, it does address the resilience of application logic. Disk, platform, and network reliability can be addressed through redundancy; but it is in the application logic that client/server systems need the most help.

This is where Java technology provides the final link in the development of a highly available system. Java programming delivers a tremendous improvement over traditional languages such as C and C++ in developing robust and reliable applications. The Java language provides several features that go a long way in developing highly available client/server applications. These features include:

- *Error handling.* The Java language provides a powerful and simple approach to identifying and capturing errors. Application developers are able to design specific error-handling routines for specific sections of program

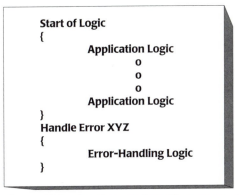

```
Start of Logic
{
            Application Logic
                   o
                   o
                   o
            Application Logic
}
Handle Error XYZ
{
            Error-Handling Logic
}
```

Figure 16.2   Java's error-handling approach

logic. Java's error-handling facilities make it much easier to consistently trap error conditions and perform retry/recovery logic without user intervention. The error handling in the Java language is a powerful tool in resolving production application logic failures. The ability to see the logic path that resulted in an application error is often critical for rapid identification and resolution of defects. Overall, this has the effect of reducing and standardizing the error-handling logic that developers have to write. Figure 16.2 is an example of a Java application's error handling.

• *Application logic trace.* The Java language provides powerful trace facilities that track the path of application logic. Used in conjunction with error handling, the application trace information provides developers with a tool that helps them better understand logic defects. Valuable development and production support time is often spent in C and C++ systems re-creating error conditions and manually tracing logic paths in order to understand application logic defects.

• *Memory management.* The Java language simplifies the management of memory for the programmer, thus greatly increasing the speed of development and the quality of the application. In C or C++, business application developers struggle with memory usage and spend significant amounts of time resolving memory problems. In many cases, the problems are not always caught during development and show up in production, resulting in expensive downtime and maintenance.

• *Thread management.* The Java language supports the concept of threaded application execution (see Figure 16.3). The concept is that an application

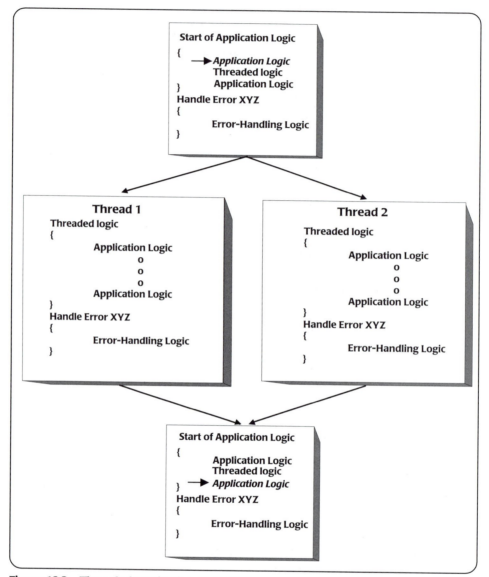

Figure 16.3   Threaded application execution

can have multiple copies of itself processing in parallel. One example is pricing of an airline ticket. There are multiple ways to determine the price of a ticket (round trip, one way, etc.), and all have to be performed if the lowest possible price is to be provided with confidence. It is faster to process the different scenarios in parallel than in series. Generally, threaded applications are difficult to build and are custom developed for each platform. The Java language greatly simplifies the complex technology required for successful implementation of a threaded application and thereby improves the resilience of these solutions.

- *Simpler syntax.* Java is a simpler development language than C or C++. Removing memory references simplifies application development as compared with C or C++. Java's use of objects is syntactically simpler than that of C++. By virtue of further simplification of the application developers' programming task, C developers had to spend only one week of training to learn to write applications in Java. With simpler syntax, the quality of the applications developed improves and the time required for debugging and maintenance is reduced.

- *Object-oriented features.* Through an object-oriented feature known as encapsulation, developers are allowed to access only the public interfaces of other business processes. The developers build applications within a framework called a shell. This shell acts as a black box and allows access to its functionality only through strict, clearly defined interfaces. With strict interfaces, it is much easier to analyze, control, and test the impacts of changes in application logic. Without this control, downtime often results because a change in one system has unforeseen impacts.

- *Compiler.* The Java compiler is a significant improvement over C and C++ compilers by virtue of its use of error and warning messages. Application logic developed in Java has gone through a significantly more stringent quality assurance review at compile time than its C and C++ counterparts.

- *Base classes.* The Java language has a richer set of building blocks for building a system than C or C++. These building blocks require less application development on the part of the developer and are generally free of defects.

16.4 The Travel Industry's High Availability Requirements

The travel industry has, since the early 1980s, built an infrastructure to support high-volume on-line transaction processing. This existing infrastructure does not support the ease, convenience, and functionality of modern client/server systems, but does perform reliably even under heavy load conditions. In the business of processing reservations for travelers, both the supplier and the traveler

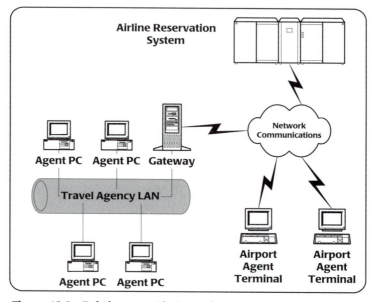

Figure 16.4   Existing travel industry infrastructure

are motivated to ensure that all systems are available to the greatest possible degree. The suppliers must have an available system if they are to generate revenue; travelers want to be sure that reservations are taken in a timely manner. Any system that attempts to improve on this infrastructure will be judged more on its availability than on its functionality and convenience. The existing infrastructure is represented in Figure 16.4.

Most of the technology components of the existing infrastructure have been around since the late 1980s. The airline agent and reservation agent terminals, the communication lines, and the mainframe computerized reservation system are components that have not changed significantly since the early 1980s. Only the local area network with client workstations and gateway servers is relatively new. Even in the case of the local area network systems, the travel industry is only beginning to adopt these configurations as they become mature technologies. The result is a highly available and tightly integrated system from which most of the bugs have been removed. This system contains the following components.

- *Agent personal computers/terminals.* These are primarily dumb terminals whose technology has not changed since the early 1980s. These devices are simple, and fail as a result of hardware problems. The other emerging user interface in the travel industry is local area network-based personal computers. These devices are more problematic because they are more complex than dumb terminals; however, the personal computers have a tested and standard configuration, and the software they use to communicate with the reservation system is relatively simple.

- *Gateway/server.* Used only in the local area network configuration, these machines talk directly to the reservation system. These machines also have a tested and standard configuration with simple communications software performing the interface with the reservation system.

- *Network communications.* Messages from the user (travel or reservation agent) to the reservation system, or vice versa, are sent over dedicated network lines connected to a centralized mainframe. These network lines are straightforward to implement and are under a high degree of sophisticated monitoring to manage the network performance and availability.

- *Reservation system mainframe.* Most travel industry computerized reservation systems are built on IBM mainframe equipment. This equipment has been tuned and tested to provide high-volume and highly reliable operation for on-line transaction processing since the early 1980s.

- *Reservation system software.* This software is generally written in IBM's Transaction Processing Facility environment. This environment and most reservation system applications were first developed in the early 1980s. This software is extremely reliable because it has been debugged and "battle tested" since its initial release.

16.5 *via* World Network's Approach

via World Network believed the existing infrastructure did not meet the needs of either the supplier of travel or the business traveler. Better processing of the traveler's reservation could reduce costs for the supplier, whereas improved time and convenience could be provided to the traveler. The challenge *via* World Network faced was the building of an Internet-based client/server system that could compete with the industry's existing infrastructure in terms of highly available transaction processing (refer to Figure 16.5). A highly available system with Internet and client/server technologies differs from the existing system in the following key characteristics:

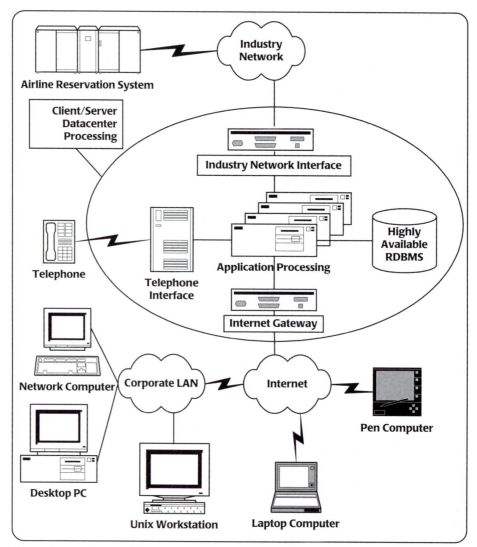

Figure 16.5 *via* **World Network's solution to building a modern, highly available system**

- *Simplicity. via* World Network was forced to integrate more components and more vendors than were present in the existing infrastructure. No longer could one supplier provide a single-vendor solution. In addition to the *via* World Network system having more components, many of its components were more complex than their counterparts in the existing industry infrastructure.

- *Control.* Whereas in the existing infrastructure the user interfaces and network lines were under the guidance and management of the overall reservation system, users of *via* World Network would require more variations to meet their needs. In many cases, it would be nearly impossible to control the user interface and the way in which users communicated to the *via* World Network reservation system.

- *Tried and true.* Components and configurations used in the *via* World Network system were based on 1990s technology. These technologies did not have the benefit of more than 20 years of tuning and debugging to "iron out" all of the bugs and defects.

Comparing the components of this system with those of the traditional system reveals the following differences.

- *User interface.* Users are no longer agents who have tested and standardized terminals or personal computers for accessing the system. Users are now business travelers who may be using their personal computers, laptops from home, personal digital assistants on the road, or the telephone to make reservations.

- *Gateway/server.* These devices allow intelligent user interface devices to access corporate networks and the Internet directly.

- *Network communications.* Dedicated lines have been replaced by multiple-use, dial-up, industry networks and the Internet. None of these networks has the monitoring and management sophistication of the traditional dedicated network connections.

- *Reservation system processing.* The reservation system is built on top of a client/server computing platform. Although this platform has a much better price/performance ratio than that of a traditional mainframe approach, multiple platforms are required to process the transaction load. In addition, a database management system is required to store transactional information.

- *Reservation system software.* The software for processing reservation transactions must be written by application developers. This software must be reliable and must manage transaction control for all user interfaces.

- *Industry infrastructure.* Seat availability for reservations must be obtained through the access of existing airline reservation systems.

In the *via* World Network case, a multivendor, redundant system strategy was coupled with the use of Java technology. This strategy resulted in a system that could compete with the existing infrastructure in terms of overall system reliability; moreover, it cost much less and could be adapted rapidly to increases in system use. Through the use of Java technology, the first two releases of the *via* World Network system experienced approximately 75 percent fewer application defects during the first six months of operation than comparable C and C++ language systems. For *via* World Network, Java technology successfully addressed the challenges of application resilience.

16.6   Summary

Often, the most successful approach to building a highly available business system involves the use of multiple technologies. Single-vendor solutions that focus on high availability, although attractive, often do not meet the requirements of the business system. Hardware and software redundancy strategies are important elements in delivering a highly available system, but they do not solve the biggest challenge—fundamental improvements in the overall resilience and quality of business process application logic. Java provides the basis for dramatic improvements in the quality of business systems by:

- Removing complexity

- Improving the implementation quality of application programs

- Providing the infrastructure for better identification and resolution of run-time errors

The key lessons learned from Java's ability to help build highly available business systems are as follows.

- Many business systems require high availability in order to service customer requirements.

- Existing strategies from single vendors and lower-cost providers focus on hardware and system software redundancy and do not address the availability of business application processing.

- Java has several features that allow businesses to develop highly available business application logic.

- The best approach is to combine the redundant hardware and system software strategy with the use of Java for application logic. This provides an end-to-end solution addressing the needs of high-availability business systems.

- Through the use of Java technology, the *via* World Network system experienced 75 percent fewer production defects in its first six months of operation than systems developed in C or C++.

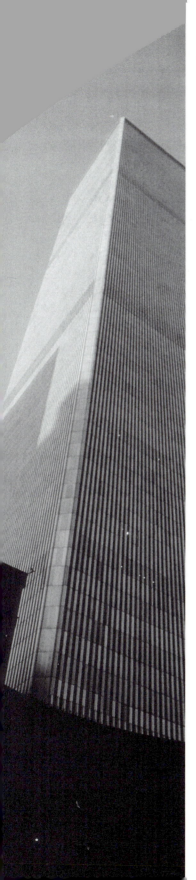

CHAPTER SEVENTEEN

Motivating Application Developers

17.1   Developers at the Java One Conference

At the end of May 1996 in San Francisco, Sun Microsystems held its first Java conference, "Java One." It was a worldwide conference with several thousand developers in attendance. (In fact, attendance was so overwhelming that some people had to be turned away.) The primary purpose of the conference was to gather developers from around the world to compare notes, form relationships, and spread the word about Java technology. The three-day conference was a series of presentations on a variety of Java topics. The presenters were software engineers who had joined the Java team in its infancy. Most of these presentations were kept short to allow maximum time for questions and answers between the audience and the presenters.

It was surprising to see the lines quickly form at the microphones as each presenter finished. Although some audience members challenged the validity and permanence of Java technology, the feelings of most were expressed by one person who went to the microphone and stated, "Before I ask my question, I just want to say thank you. Java has made my job more interesting. I am more excited about my work and what I do. You guys are doing a great job." It was a moving statement that was quietly echoed by a murmur in the audience as others agreed. There even followed brief applause for the presenters and the technology they had developed.

When this situation occurred, it seemed a bit outlandish. How could Java, a new technology, actually make someone's job better? The statement would probably have gone unnoticed except that several other people approached the microphones throughout the conference and stated virtually the same thing. There was no disputing the fact that the developers at the conference were passionate about Java. There was excitement in the air. People had Java in common and they wanted to share their experiences. They couldn't get enough of Java.

A person could argue, "Of course everyone at the conference was interested in Java; they were a group of hard-core Java developers." But when one talks with peers throughout the industry, it is evident that the interest in Java technology is widespread. Software developers around the world want to work with Java technology. A Zona Research study in mid-1997 found that the third most likely reason for a company to be experimenting in Java was developer interest.

While developers and technologists have taken a fair share of criticism for focusing exclusively on the technology and not on the business requirements, Java technology is a case where a business has the opportunity to capitalize on the interest in a technology and leverage increased work force productivity.

By following the experiences of developers on a Java project, this chapter explores the reasons why developers like Java technology and how their liking for Java technology can be leveraged by a business.

17.2 A Variety of Reasons

There is no single, overriding reason why developers are attracted to Java programming. Some of the reasons are inherent in the Java language and some are external. The following points are factors that drive developer interest in Java technology.

- Java is new and different.

- Java technology is cutting-edge.

- The industry has overhyped Java.

- Java programming is easy to learn.

- Animated web pages.

- Java technology increases prototyping speed.

- Sharing of Java code.

- Excitement over the Internet.

17.2.1 Java Is New and Different

Most of the languages currently used in the software industry are considered "old" in computer technology time. C, C++, COBOL, and others have been around for ten to 20 years. Many software developers are looking for something new, and Java programming is the answer. Java technology was first released in the spring of 1995, and the first production release took place in the spring of 1996.

Whenever something new impacts the software industry with strong backing and attention, developers want to understand what is behind the new technology. The interest in Java technology among its core supporters encourages other developers to want to learn more. Developers have heard about Java technology and that it has interesting, powerful new programming and Internet-integration capabilities.

17.2.2 Java Technology Is Cutting-Edge

Cutting-edge technology can be defined as a technology that has not yet proven itself in major production applications, but has demonstrated the potential to deliver significant benefits. Both the allure and the risk of a new technology drive many developers to Java technology, much as wilderness and uncharted waters drive explorers. Cutting-edge technology is the gateway to the future, and software developers are looking for ways to break ahead of the pack with new technologies and new ideas.

Java programming has demonstrated powerful possibilities for the future of computing. To many it appears to be the answer to some difficult problems. It has the potential to change software development as we know it. For a developer, the chance to work with Java technology is a chance to explore the future.

17.2.3 The Industry Has Overhyped Java

Java technology has been overhyped. Articles about Java technology in the press and in general business and industry publications are frequent and in some cases have overstated the potential of the technology. Some people are going so far as to state that Java technology is a revolution in the software industry, a panacea for software development problems. Although Java technology has been overhyped, there have been kernels of truth at the heart of many of the claims.

Whether warranted or not, the hype has a powerful impact on software developers. Once they have heard about the wonderful features of Java programming, it is difficult to keep application developers from being pulled along by the excitement.

17.2.4 Java Programming Is Easy to Learn

Because Java programming is easy to learn, programmers can become productive in the Java language in a short period of time. It is so easy to learn that the home experimenter can focus on having fun and creating exciting, simple applications. Since the Java Development Kit (JDK) can be downloaded from the Internet at no cost, developers can experiment with Java programming without having to purchase expensive tools.

Knowing that the barrier to entry into the Java development world is low encourages developers to take time (often personal time) to investigate Java technology. Once they investigate it, developers of all levels often become "hooked" as they realize how fast they can create simple applications.

17.2.5 Animated Web Pages

When the popular browsers made it quick and easy for developers around the world to access the Web, Internet development took off. Millions of people around the world became involved in Web development. The primary technology used for creating applications on the Web is HyperText Markup Language (HTML). HTML allows a developer to quickly and easily create a window with graphics and text. Web developers can quickly create a story, attach a picture, and display it to anyone. Development using HTML has gone from nonexistent to omnipresent in a few short years. In many ways, the reasons for developers' interest in HTML are similar to the reasons for their interest in Java.

There was something missing from Web development, however. There is little excitement in a static screen of text and graphics on which user interaction is limited. If the pictures could move and if people could watch a story play out in front of them and have increased interaction with the application, the interest and usefulness of applications on the Internet would dramatically increase.

This is why there was so much excitement when Java was originally introduced. Most of the initial Java applications were simple, fun, animated GUI programs, which quickly caught the attention of Web software developers. Although the ability to animate applications and add interesting graphics already existed, Java technology made these activities easier and more feasible, especially over the Internet. This strategy was wise, because as GUI applications and animation are interesting to a wide range of developers. Had the promoters of Java technology initially focused on back-end programs that processed complex logic but were not "fun," the interest in Java applications would have been significantly less.

17.2.6 Java Increases Prototyping Speed

Because the Java language is a simpler language than C or C++ and comes pre-packaged with building blocks for the application, it is an ideal language to use for prototyping. A developer new to Java programming can create a GUI application in a matter of hours and see the work materialize very quickly. The ability to achieve quick, tangible results is a strong reason for developer interest in Java technology.

17.2.7 Sharing of Java Code

The Java community is open and encourages cooperation. Sun Microsystems has released the source code for the Java language and tools that come with the JDK. Because Java technology was conceived with openness in mind, Java developers are sharing more code than typically has been shared in the past. There are Internet sites on which implementers can place their code for others to use. Developers appreciate the open nature of Java development because it allows them to take advantage of each other's work.

17.2.8 Excitement over the Internet

Much of the foreseeable future of computing will revolve around the Internet. Electronic commerce and other Internet-based applications are the direction of companies around the world. Estimates vary, but technology analysts agree that there will be billions of dollars spent on Internet development as well as billions of dollars of commerce over the Internet by the year 2000.

One of the problems facing companies is that technology is struggling to keep up with the expectations and wishes of visionaries. There are issues involving security, performance, implementation time, and flexibility of the applications. These issues have slowed the momentum of Internet development, and companies are hesitant to commit large resources to Web-based applications. Many are waiting for others to take the leap first, hoping to benefit from the inevitable mistakes and successes of others.

Java technology is one of the first tools created for Internet-based applications. It directly addresses many of the issues related to the Web. Java gives companies confidence of success, and thus they are more willing to make the conversion to Java technology. Because the Java language was meant to be a Web-based development platform and language, it has become one of the first technologies that developers look to for ideas. New and experienced developers alike want to be involved in the Web, and the tie between Java technology and the Internet increases their interest in Java.

17.3   Developers Are Motivated to Work with Java Technology

It is apparent that developers like working with Java applications, but what does this mean to a company? It has often happened that company management has been persuaded by technologists to use a particular technology they found technically interesting and were convinced would meet their business requirements. Unfortunately, too many times such projects have fallen drastically behind schedule or have completely failed because of too much focus on technology and not enough on business requirements. It is all too common to fall into this technology trap and be led down an expensive, difficult path that does not provide the promised business benefits.

If not properly controlled, the excitement over Java technology can cause the same problems. However, realistic expectations for Java development can translate into the following benefits:

- Developers work harder.

- Recruiting is easier.

- Developers have a positive attitude.

- Developers establish personal contacts with other Java developers.

17.3.1 Developers Work Harder

If people are interested in what they are doing, they work harder, produce higher-quality work, and complete their tasks faster. If they are bored or uninterested, they produce substandard work and take longer to produce it. It is quite common for people to work longer hours with more effort when they enjoy what they are doing. Experience suggests that Java generates strong enthusiasm, which leads to higher levels of interest and passion than similar C or C++ projects inspire.

17.3.2 Recruiting Is Easier

It is difficult (if not impossible) to hire talented developers for support positions in legacy systems. Highly talented developers tend to accept positions within companies either for the exciting, new technology or because they are interested in a state-of-the-art project the company is undertaking. Usually, these developers do not want to support old technology and do not want to maintain what they view as an archaic system.

Java development is an emerging and exciting technology. This sparks the interest of developers and draws them to opportunities that will allow them to use Java technology on a daily basis. Based on this overwhelming interest in Java development, a company's decision to use the Java platform and language will give it a competitive edge for recruiting the best and brightest developers.

17.3.3 Developers Have a Positive Attitude

Developers working on Java applications have a positive attitude about their work and their work environment. Java development is new, exciting, and fun, and developers find it challenging. When developers on a legacy system using technology that has been around for 20 years are transferred to a new project being developed in Java technology, in most cases their attitudes towards work will improve. This situation has never been more apparent than at the Java One conference, where everyone attending was glad to be developing Java applications and shared the belief that Java had made their jobs more interesting.

17.3.4 Developers Establish Professional Contacts

Java developers are a community. They have the common trait of enjoying their work with Java technology. Because of their common source of enjoyment and the openness of the Java world, they naturally communicate with each other. They establish relationships, exchange ideas, and form friendships. Java developers establish professional relationships with other Java developers from all over the world. There is a flow of information between them as new ideas and challenges are uncovered during development of Java applications. This flow of information enables additional productivity as relationships help uncover solutions to and strategies for application development challenges.

17.4   Experiences with the Interest in Java

At its peak of application development, *via* World Network had approximately 100 application developers and technical support personnel. Until January 1996, *via* World Network was targeting a C++/PowerBuilder platform. At the end of January, Java technology was a popular media subject and had become one of the most exciting industry technologies. *via* World Network management had concluded its research into the Java technology and had made the decision that it was a viable platform for deploying applications. Once Java development had been approved, the technology team began working on the infrastructure to support application development. About 20 people from the company participated in the creation of a Java application development infrastructure. The team's responsibility was to learn and master the Java language, then use the language to create a framework on which the rest of the company could develop business applications.

The most noticeable change initially brought about by Java technology was an increased interest in the work being performed. Not only was the team building a state-of-the-art system in the airline industry, they were building it using the latest and greatest available software technology. Being part of a company that had decided to build its future on Java technology was exciting for those closest to the implementation. The technical team quickly became aware of the benefits of Java technology and also the risks *via* World Network was assuming. Despite the tight deadlines and overtime, the team members remained upbeat because they were interested in and passionate about the new technology.

The team not only worked with a positive attitude but also took their excitement outside of the project. They frequently explained their work to others and were often asked if the company was looking for additional help.

The outside interest that was brewing is best illustrated by an experience of two technology team members. Two of the primary architects of the system attended a meeting of a small software discussion group in Minneapolis. The discussion group met periodically to discuss advances in and implementations using object-oriented technology. Eventually, the two team members from *via* World Network had an opportunity to present. They planned to give a high-level overview of the project and of the technology used, not a detailed explanation of their use of Java technology. No sooner had they started their presentation when they were flooded with questions about building Java applications. The group was extremely interested in details, and the two presenters spent the next couple of hours discussing only Java technology. This incident raised the spirits of the two architects even higher and added fuel to the fire when they related the experience to the rest of the team.

On the recruiting front, Java development helped bring talented people onto the team. At the time, recruiting in the software industry was extremely difficult. The demand for talented software developers was high, and the available people were demanding premium salaries and titles. Once the decision to use Java technology was final, recruiting for the company changed. Neither pay nor position was the most important factor for recruits. Instead, they were most intrigued by the use of Java technology and requested to be allowed to work with it. Some of the people accepted the jobs for the sole reason that they would be working closely with Java applications if hired. The opportunity to work with Java technology was not used as the primary selling point for the recruits, but it was clear that developers in the software industry were interested in working with it.

The developers enjoyed the challenges, new features, and visibility of Java technology as well as the intrigue of the exploration. From the beginning, the developers knew the risks of building Java applications, but this only added to their intensity. The use of Java technology was not a primary reason for *via* World Network's success; however, Java development had positive influences on the organization's morale, the speed at which people worked, and the quality of the finished product.

17.5 Summary

Committing a company's developers to a particular technology may or may not benefit the organization. Excitement over a new technology may cause a company to make poor business decisions, because strategies should be based on business benefits and not on technology intrigue. If the interest in Java technology is appropriately placed, software developers will appreciate the opportunity to develop applications in Java, and the company may well see benefits in morale, productivity, and quality. Key considerations regarding developer interest in Java technology are as follows.

- Software developers like Java development for a variety of reasons, including the excitement of a new technology, Java's ease of learning, its integration with the Web/Internet, and the opportunity to build applications leveraging its rich functionality.

- The interest in Java can be leveraged by companies to increase productivity, attract better employees, and improve morale.

- *via* World Network is an example of a business that was able to leverage developer interest in Java to improve its delivery of a complex business system.

CHAPTER EIGHTEEN

Learning the Technology

18.1 The Cost of Training

A significant cost for companies is the expense of training information systems software developers. Software developers are typically required to learn multiple programming languages throughout their careers. When a new employee is hired or an existing employee is staffed on a new project, time and money must be invested before the new team member can be expected to be productive. New team members must be trained in the development process, the business process, and their administrative responsibilities. Additional time and expense are incurred if the developers must learn a new programming language. The time it takes to learn a new language varies for each individual, but it is generally measured in weeks and months, not in days. Even if a developer has worked with the programming language but on a different platform, she or he must learn the differences in the language on the new platform (for example, learning C on a UNIX workstation after using it on a Microsoft Windows PC).

The Java language is a solution to this problem. The Java language is a simplified, full-featured, object-oriented programming language that is independent of computing platform and has syntax similar to yet easier than those of existing popular languages such as C and C++. Because Java development is easier to learn and is platform independent, training developers in Java is less time-consuming and less expensive than training them in other languages.

This chapter explores why Java is easier to learn than C or C++ for both experienced and inexperienced application developers. In addition, tips for training developers and the experience gained in a large software development project are presented.

18.2 Java Is Easier to Learn

Software developers typically master more than one programming language during their careers. As additional languages are mastered, it becomes easier and easier to learn new languages. Listed below are reasons why Java is easier to learn than other popular programming languages such as C and C++. These reasons apply to developers of all levels, although the impact varies with experience.

- Simpler syntax

- Similarity to C and C++

- Wide base of documentation

- Prebuilt building blocks

- Simpler memory management

- User-friendly compiler

- Platform independence

- Simplified systems programming

- Simplified object-oriented programming

18.2.1 Simpler Syntax

The most widely used programming language in the business world is COBOL. Distant followers, but still used in many applications, are C and C++. The inventors of Java technology were well aware of C and C++ and knew their advantages and disadvantages. One of the most important objectives of the Java language was to keep it simple. Java's creators borrowed from existing, common programming constructs where possible. Whenever they had to deviate from existing programming languages, they chose easy-to-understand syntax.

In the Java language, even the most complex features have a simple syntax. Concepts that traditionally took several lines of complex C or C++ code now take only a single line of code in Java. Examples include complex synchronization of applications, communicating across the network, and communicating with a user in a GUI application. This simplified approach creates a sort of pseudo-language that makes it easier to develop applications than in a C or C++ environment.

Another simplifying feature of the Java syntax is a reduction in programming choices. In a language such as C or C++, the programmer can code each statement in a variety of ways, whereas in the Java language, the number of ways to program a given statement has been reduced. Examples include character string manipulation and memory management. Because of the reduced number of alternative methods of accomplishing the same objective, the Java developer is less confused and has fewer commands to master.

18.2.2 Similarity to C and C++

Investment in C and C++ skills is preserved, because the Java syntax was based on these languages. All of the simple, common programmatic constructs in C and C++ remain unchanged in Java, allowing experienced programmers to begin programming simple applications in Java immediately. Experienced programmers spend little time learning the basics and therefore can focus their efforts on learning the more advanced features of the Java language.

18.2.3 Wide Base of Documentation

One of the most important things for a company to consider when deciding whether or not to use a new technology is documentation. Without proper documentation, development is a painful, time-consuming activity of trial and error. Despite the fact that Java is still in its infancy, people around the world have already created a tremendous amount of Java reference material. There are hundreds of programming books written about the Java language. The Internet contains thousands of pages of information about Java development and examples of its use. This is an advantage for both experienced and inexperienced application developers.

18.2.4 Prebuilt Building Blocks

Large system development using existing programming languages generally requires the creation of a set of common routines (for example, communications, date, and string routines) to be used by all business application developers. These routines are created to ensure consistent implementation and to save time in business application development. Before significant business application development can begin, this base set of routines must be designed, created, and tested. These foundation building blocks must be solid, because problems in these common routines will propagate throughout most of the business application. Creating these basic building blocks for a system generally requires several days of work by the technical developers as they attempt to create a robust set of common modules.

The Java language reduces the need for this step in development. It provides basic, common routines that developers have created over and over on projects throughout the world. Some examples are a String class that provides many common string functions, a Date class that provides many common date functions, and a Vector class that provides common array functions.

These building blocks will take the experienced programmer little time to master. They are consistent with previous programming languages and provide a simple interface. For new developers, the time required to learn how to use these building blocks is no more than it takes to read a Java manual. New and experienced developers alike will benefit from the Java language's common routines.

18.2.5 Simpler Memory Management

The most difficult and time-consuming technique to master in languages such as C and C++ is the use of memory pointers. Their confusing, convoluted syntax is extremely difficult to read and understand. It generally takes years for most business application programmers to master the use of memory pointers.

One of the most important features of the Java language is the elimination of memory pointers. For this feature alone, Java is worth using on development projects. There are many advantages of eliminating the use of memory pointers, not the least of which is reduced learning time for developers. Because pointers are eliminated, learning the basics of Java takes half the time required to learn C or C++.

The impact of eliminating pointers is especially beneficial to new programmers. Generally, the concept of pointers is not completely taught to new programmers at universities or in professional training sessions. Instead, programmers are taught all the other basics first, and only when they have become somewhat familiar with the language is the concept of pointers studied. The entire step of learning pointers is eliminated in the Java language.

Typically, experienced programmers have had to worry about memory allocation and have carefully managed their use of memory. Despite this background, experienced programmers invest days or even weeks learning memory pointers for a new programming language. This training time is zero with Java technology.

18.2.6 User-Friendly Compiler

One of the fundamental tools of a software developer is a compiler. The compiler is a tool that takes application statements and turns them into a program that can be executed. Typically, a developer turns code into an executable program dozens of times each day using the compiler.

When a compiler is executed, it first searches through the developer's code and checks for syntax errors. If an error is encountered, the compiler gives the developer a message and stops compiling. If no errors are detected, the compiler creates a file that can be executed.

There are two benefits of the Java compiler over existing compilers. The first advantage is its thorough detection of errors. Because the Java language has simpler syntax and stricter programing rules than those of other languages, the Java compiler can be more intelligent about detecting programming mistakes. Not only will the compiler catch all of the syntax mistakes caught by current compilers, but it will also catch those hard-to-detect errors that are usually missed. Such errors can take several hours to debug once the program has been executed. The best example of an error not caught by C or C++ compilers but caught by the Java compiler is a single rather than double equal sign in an "if" statement, such as "if (x = y)" instead of "if (x == y)." The first is usually a programming error, and the second is correct. C and C++ compilers allow both statements, but Java flags the first as an error, which can save hours of programming time.

The other advantage of the Java compiler is the clarity of its error messages to the developer. Many non-Java compilers generate erroneous or vague messages when errors are encountered. Because of the simplicity of the Java language (compared with C or C++), the Java compiler can generate more informative error messages.

The Java compiler allows both experienced and inexperienced developers to begin programming without fully understanding all of the syntax rules of Java and without worrying about making mistakes. The compiler catches errors and generates detailed messages explaining them. This provides developers with accurate feedback and allows them to quickly create syntactically correct code. Less time is spent deciphering vague compiler messages or debugging bad code the compiler should have caught, and thus the developer has more time to learn the Java language.

18.2.7 Platform Independence

The platform dependence of existing programming languages promotes complexity in software development. An application that is platform dependent must be modified to execute on a different machine and operating system. The differences from platform to platform may be minor, but the process of learning and understanding these differences consumes developers' time and leads to problems with writing, compiling, and executing code.

The developers of Java technology addressed the issue of platform dependence. A core theme of Java technology was to allow companies the ability to create applications that were not dependent on the underlying technology (see Figure 18.1).

Java technology has not completely fulfilled the goal of platform independence. It has come a long way toward the vision, but applications executing on different platforms do not always behave the same, especially when dealing with user interfaces. A window created on one platform does not always appear in the same shape and layout on another platform. The differences are minor and in some cases unnoticeable; however, the development team should be careful to test the platform independence of applications that are deployed to multiple platforms.

For the most part, Java technology's attempt at platform independence has eliminated the platform-dependent problems in languages such as C and C++. Platform independence decreases the amount of time required of both new and experienced developers when the deployment platform changes.

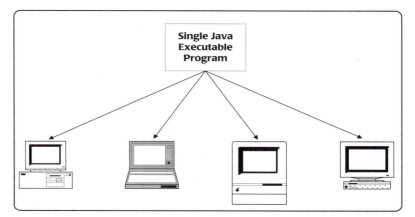

Figure 18.1   Platform-independent Java

18.2.8 Simplified Systems Programming

Complex programming tasks that typically deal with low-level programming interfaces have been dubbed "systems programming." Systems programming refers to the creation of programs that interface with external sources such as hardware, operating systems, databases, and networks. Systems programming includes concepts such as synchronization of the processing of multiple applications, communication over a network to another program, and interfacing with the operating system. These complex tasks are addressed only by more experienced programmers and take years to understand completely and to master. Most large projects require systems programming; unfortunately, hiring someone who is effective at systems programming is expensive, and training someone takes time.

The creators of the Java language knew how complex these types of programming activities are and how important they are to large systems. While creating the Java language, they implemented easy-to-use programming constructs that aid in systems programming. Both new and experienced programmers save time learning how to perform complex systems programming in the Java language.

18.2.9 Simplified Object-Oriented Programming

The most popular programming technique in the software industry today is object-oriented programming. Chapter 11 discusses object development and some of its advantages and disadvantages. Object development on a large system is difficult to understand for new programmers without object-oriented training; object concepts are numerous and difficult to comprehend.

Even though Java is an object-oriented language, it reduces object-oriented complexity as compared with other languages, such as C++. The Java language enforces rules of programming that simplify many object techniques. By virtue of reduced object complexity, new developers spend less time learning advanced object development techniques and more time building applications. Experienced object developers find that even though the Java language has simplified object programming, it still has all the advantages of an object language.

18.2.10 Impact of Java on New and Experienced Developers

Table 18.1 summarizes the reasons why the Java language is easy to learn and its impacts on both new and experienced developers.

Table 18.1   Impact on new and experienced developers

Reason	Impact on New Developers	Impact on Experienced Developers
Simpler syntax	Major	Minor
Syntax similar to C/C++	Minor	Major
Documentation	None	Minor
Building blocks	Major	Major
No memory pointers	Major	Major
Java compiler	Major	Minor
Platform independence	Major	Major
Systems programming	Major	Major
Easier object development	Major	Minor
Developers prefer Java	Major	Major

18.3   Learning Java Still Takes Time

The time it takes to learn the Java language is less than the time it takes to learn a language such as C++, but it is expensive to train developers in any new language, even Java. Learning how to be a good programmer remains a difficult task. Companies planning to use Java technology should plan on investing a significant amount of time (two to four weeks) for application developer training.

18.4   *via* World Network Training

When the decision was made to use the Java language on *via* World Network, not one of the 100 team members knew how to program in Java. *via* World Network had new programmers, experienced programmers, and every level in between. There were a few developers with more than ten years of experience in programming in a variety of languages, most had two to three years of C or COBOL programming, and about a third had little or no programming experience. Out of the 100 developers, only about five had significant object-oriented programming experience. The educational backgrounds of the team members varied in content and level. The majority of team members had business information systems backgrounds. Many of the others had math, computer science, or engineering backgrounds, whereas a few had liberal arts or teaching degrees. All in all, the project team was diverse and had very few technical "gurus."

The overall development team was divided into two groups of developers: the technical team and the functional team. The technical team focused on technically challenging tasks such as database access and network communications. The functional team focused on the business application and leveraging the routines provided by the technical team to complete their programs.

To solve the problem of bringing 100 team members up to speed on Java programming, the technical team first addressed Java application development. There were about 20 technical team members who studied books on the Java language and began programming simple Java applications. The project sent a few people to take Sun Microsystem's Java programming course. The technical team also browsed the Internet for examples of Java applications.

Once the technical team members had become familiar with the language, they began to create the application framework for the project. They developed programming standards, program shells, development tools, and application support libraries. These libraries became the foundation of the execution architecture (refer to Chapter 12). At the point at which the development infrastructure started to take shape, the developers were ready to begin coding. Everything was in place except that not one functional developer knew how to create a Java program and some of them had never programmed in any language.

To leverage their Java skills to the functional team, the technical team members led training sessions. Approximately ten people were responsible for researching, creating training materials, and presenting. A training expert was brought in to ensure that the training was consistent and well prepared, and that the trainers were ready for their presentations. Training preparation took about two weeks. At the end of preparation, the project had a 200-page course binder with slides, code examples, exercises, and pictures.

Two training sessions were held about two weeks apart, with each session having 30 to 40 attendees. The attendees consisted of new developers, experienced developers, managers, project leads, and technical team members new to Java programming. The training was tailored to individuals with no experience with Java programming or the technical environment. A wide variety of topics were covered in a short period of time.

- A brief introduction to object programming was covered in two hours (refer to Chapter 11 for why this introduction was so brief).

- Java programming basics were covered in four hours.

- Programming in the development environment and execution architecture were covered in about twenty hours.

- Finally, developers worked on example exercises. These exercises provided the developers with a quick test of their knowledge of Java programming.

After the first two-week training course, developers were ready to try their hands at programming business applications. Immediately after the first training session, the trained developers were coding Java applications. After the second training session, the entire development team was programming. Within two months after completing the training, every project member had done some form of Java programming. Only a few developers required additional training, and all were able to build their assigned applications effectively. In six months, the functional developers created a complex application with more than 3,700 function points (more than 200,000 lines of Java code).

After the first release of the application, the technical team surveyed the developers about the effectiveness of their training. One of the new developers questioned had only two weeks of C programming before joining the project. He believed that the training had been invaluable to the extent that he would not have been productive without it. He believed that Java programming was easier to learn than C, and he praised the Java language and touted its benefits over C. Other more experienced functional developers echoed these beliefs.

18.5   Training Tips

To help companies train developers, a list of training tips that have been collected from multiple Java projects is presented below. This list offers helpful hints on how to get a team up to speed and productive with Java programming.

- Make use of the information on the Web. It is free, is easy to access, and is the most up-to-date. The best place to start is www.javasoft.com.

- Purchase a few Java programming books.

- Not all developers need to be sent to classes. Save money by sending a few team members and have them relay the important points to the rest of the team.

- Have the experienced developers create exercises for the others. This will help both the experienced and inexperienced programmers.

- Make use of the compiler, relying on its error detection and messages.

- The best way to learn Java programming is to work with it. It is simple enough for developers to start programming immediately. Have each developer grab a book, log onto the system, and learn.

18.6 Summary

Java development benefits a company by reducing the time and effort required to be productive in a new programming language. It is important, however, to develop a well-planned training agenda to introduce developers to the major Java programming concepts. Through the use of Java books and resources such as the Web, developers will quickly come up to speed and become effective at creating Java applications. Key considerations in training application developers in Java are as follows.

- Training both inexperienced and experienced application developers is expensive and time consuming.

- It takes less time for inexperienced and experienced developers alike to become productive in building applications in Java than in C or C++.

- Learning Java programming, although relatively quick, still takes some time and should be supported with a well-organized training plan.

- The following simple training tips will help a company go a long way in developing Java skills.
  - Leverage the information available on the Web.
  - Review and select appropriate Java programming books.
  - Send a few developers to Java classes and leverage this investment to all developers.
  - Have more experienced developers create exercises for less experienced personnel.
  - Examine the Java compiler output for programming tips.
  - Have developers dive in and start learning through experimentation.

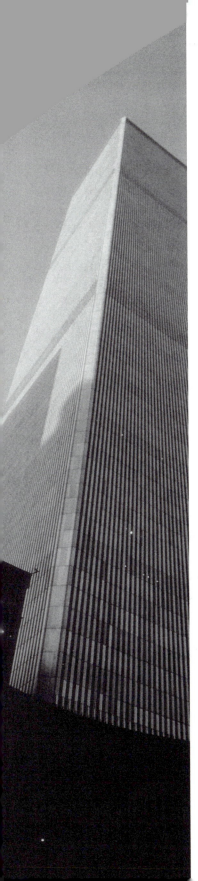

CHAPTER NINETEEN

Improving Developer Productivity

19.1 Programming Is a Complex, Time-Consuming Task

The clock has just struck midnight, and as each hour passes you feel a little more concerned. The team has been working on a program for two weeks and is now one week behind. You are responsible for the team and their work. You've worked with this team and you know how good they are, but it still is frustrating that even after all this time the team is falling behind because of programming problems.

Sound familiar? When you stop and think about it, it is surprising that, as far as software development technology has evolved, systems development is still plagued with the problems that have existed for decades. In *The Mythical Man Month*, Frederick Brooks discusses improvements in programming languages. He evaluates how different programming languages and tools have evolved over time, and the impact each change has had on the programmer's job. Over the last few decades, programmers have enjoyed only incremental improvements in productivity as application development has remained a difficult task. There has been no "silver bullet" in the software industry that has effected a significant reduction in the time and complexity involved in programming. This is especially true for complex business system projects that require large numbers of developers.

19.2 Java Programming Increases Developer Productivity

When people first learn Java technology, one of their first remarks is, "Wow, why didn't *we* think of this?" The creators of Java technology looked back at the last 20 years of software development, learned from past mistakes, and created a modern programming language. Finally, there is a way to avoid common problems that have faced developers for years. The technology used in the Java language is not new. Java technology has incorporated a number of good ideas, has brought them together into a solution resembling popular development languages such as C and C++, and has received the backing of major vendors within the information technology industry (Sun Microsystems, IBM, HP, Oracle, Microsoft, and so on).

Table 19.1 is a comparison of Java with other programming languages. This comparison was published by Sun Microsystems. It is a good starting point for comparing and contrasting the Java language with other languages. For several reasons, Java technology has the ability to help application developers be more productive. Once developers have become familiar with the language, there is a strong possibility that they will produce better code, faster. The level of productivity will not double, but it should improve.

The comparisons made in this chapter are between developers coding in C and COBOL and developers coding in Java. These comparisons are based on the first two production releases developed for *via* World Network between

Table 19.1   Java versus other languages

	Java	SmallTalk	TCL	Perl	Shells	C	C++
Simple	●	●	●	◐	◐	◐	○
Object Oriented	●	●	○	●	○	○	◐
Robust	●	●	●	●	●	○	○
Secure	●	◐	◐	●	◐	○	○
Interpreted	●	●	●	●	●	○	○
Dynamic	●	●	●	●	◐	○	○
Portable	●	◐	●	●	◐	◐	◐
Neutral	●	◐	◐	●	◐	○	○
Threads	●	○	○	●	○	○	○
Garbage Collection	●	●	○	○	○	○	○
Exceptions	●	●	○	●	○	○	◐
Performance	High	Medium	Low	Medium	Low	High	High

● Feature exists

◐ Feature somewhat exists

○ Feature doesn't exist

March 1996 and February 1997. During this time, *via* World Network developed a travel management application with more than 800,000 lines of code and measuring more than 15,000 function points in application complexity. This system performed pricing, booking, and refunding of domestic United States electronic tickets. By March 1997, *via* World Network was seeing significant productivity and quality improvements over application development in C or C++ (Table 19.2).

These improvements can be traced to Java's impacts in the areas of:

• Memory management

• Compiler

• Base classes

• Systems programming

• Platform independence

• Object-oriented programming

• Error handling

19.2.1 Memory Management

Throughout the history of software development, programmers have worried about managing a computer's memory. It started in the 1960s, when programmers were confined to only a few kilobytes of memory. Each byte of memory was important, and if one were wasted it could have a major impact on the feasibility of the application. Today, the amount of memory available to applications has increased dramatically, and developers no longer need to optimize the use of every byte.

Table 19.2   *via* World Network productivity/quality improvements

Stage	Java Impact	Comments
Coding/unit testing	10% reduction in time	Compared with C/Cobol estimates
System testing	20% reduction in time	Compared with C/Cobol estimates
First six months of production operations	75% reduction in defects	Compared with C/Cobol operations

However, despite the dramatic increase in memory available to each computer, developers still have to be careful not to consume too much memory. For example, if a program wastes only a few bytes of data each minute but runs for days, it will eventually consume all of its memory, resulting in its failure.

Today, languages such as C and C++ require the developer to manage memory usage. Programmers are responsible for allocating and freeing memory. If they do not free all allocated memory or if they make mistakes and incorrectly use memory, their programs will abort. Problems such as these are called memory leaks or memory faults. Appropriate memory management in a large, complex application is time-consuming to program and debug. The nontechnical business application developer will spend more time on memory management than on any other programming activity.

Whenever a program allocates memory, it references the area of memory using what is called a pointer. The pointer "points" to the area of memory so that the program can reference this location. This sounds easy, but is quite complex and is a leading cause of program defects in business applications. Often a program does not allocate a large enough area in memory and attempts to store more data than the memory can hold. This data will overwrite other information in memory, causing the application to abort. This problem is difficult to detect, because the program does not abort when the memory is allocated. It may not even fail when the memory is overwritten. But it usually fails some time later when the program tries to reference the information that has been overwritten. These types of problems are difficult to solve, and can take days for an experienced technical programmer to analyze.

The Java language implements a commonsense approach to memory allocation and the problems associated with pointers. Instead of having the developer worry about memory management, the Java language performs this function. There are no pointers in the Java language. The Java virtual machine allocates and frees the memory an application needs. The developer defines variables and indicates when to allocate space. The Java virtual machine determines how much to allocate and ensures that memory will not be accidentally overwritten. When variables are no longer used, the Java virtual machine automatically cleans up the memory space. Using this approach, the Java language eliminates a major contributor to defects and reduced application developer productivity. This alone makes business application developers noticeably more productive by saving time in both programming and debugging.

19.2.2 Compiler

When developers finish writing code, they turn their code into an executable program using a compiler. The compiler reads the code to find any errors. If there are errors, the compiler informs the developer of the mistakes. If there are no errors, the compiler creates an executable program. This is an activity that is performed several times a day by developers.

There are two primary problems with existing C and C++ compilers: the compilers do not always give accurate error information, and they do not always catch potential problems.

By communicating more meaningful messages and performing tighter error checking on the code, the Java compiler actually increases the productivity of developers. Instead of tracking down vague syntax problems or debugging the program, Java developers can quickly locate and fix problems identified by the compiler. Fixing a clearly communicated error at compile time takes much less time than locating and fixing a vague error at runtime.

19.2.3 Base Classes

Base classes are programmatic building blocks that are common to most applications. These classes perform functions such as manipulating dates, communicating over networks, and storing collections of related data. Base classes are important to projects with several developers because they establish a common set of routines that will be shared, saving development time and making system development more consistent across applications. The Java language comes prepackaged with several base classes; thus, projects using Java technology start ahead of those that use languages such as C and C++.

The Java language eliminates the time required to develop these classes, and also eliminates the time required to debug and test this functionality. The provision of base classes is a powerful advantage. It is vital that common routines used by the project team be robust and error free. When using a base class, an application developer generally assumes that the base class works and that the problem is in the application code. Errors in base classes result in hours spent debugging code. After several hours, the developer gets help from the author of the base class, and after a few more hours the problem is found. Unfortunately, this is all too common a problem in large business systems development. A bug in a base class has a magnified impact on the overall application development team. With the Java language, the base classes have been fully debugged and are used by thousands of developers around the world.

In some cases, the base classes provided by the Java language can save additional time by illustrating ideas that developers may not have otherwise conceived. If a developer examines the base classes in the Java language, he or she may find methods that are needed but would not have expected to be there. Before a project team begins creating an application, the team should carefully study all of the classes provided by the Java language.

Comparatively, C and C++ do not provide such a rich set of base classes or common routines. Filling this void by providing a rich set of base classes is a fundamental component of Java technology and is another reason why Java developers are able to show productivity gains over development in C or C++.

19.2.4 Systems Programming

In large corporate development projects (generally requiring more than 20 people for more than one year), most of the application developers focus on the business logic of the system. This means they are focused on, for example, ensuring that the system appropriately prices a ticket, updates customer information, or updates inventory. Business logic is comprised of line after line of simple statements that, as a whole, process business transactions. If a technically difficult programming task is required, the developers coding business logic use routines provided by more technical programmers, often organized into a technical team. The technical team provides the other developers with common routines for complex tasks. This arrangement leverages common technical routines across the project and requires that only a few of the project's programmers have deep technical skills.

Programming technically complex routines is called systems programming. Systems programmers deal with challenging technical issues and must have a good understanding of the underlying operating system and hardware. Examples of systems programming include database access, network communications, security, and multiple application synchronization. Once the systems programmer has completed coding of these challenging routines, the routines are rolled out to the rest of the development team.

Obviously, systems programming is difficult and time-consuming. The Java language does not eliminate the need for systems programming, but it does minimize much of the effort involved. The Java language attempts to complete as much of this complex work as possible in a generic manner by including numerous classes to support the systems programmer. These classes go a long way toward reducing the workload of the systems programmer.

In addition to being friendly to systems programmers, Java's support for systems programming also saves time for business application developers relying on technical routines. As with base classes, the typical developer assumes that the underlying technical classes are correct. If these classes do not work, the application developer spends hours trying to resolve the problem and eventually calls in the technical author. The problem is compounded, however, in routines created by the systems programmer, because the code is much more complex. It can take weeks to solve problems in complex technical routines in a system. Because the work of systems programmers is reduced, a corresponding gain in productivity is realized by business application developers. Fewer lines of custom systems programming code result in fewer bugs to delay the application developers.

19.2.5 Platform Independence

Today's common programming languages are available on all major platforms. For example, developers can code in C on a Sun/UNIX machine or an IBM personal computer running OS/2. Unfortunately, application development on these platforms requires routines that are specific to the platform. A C program written on a Sun/UNIX machine will most likely require modification to run successfully on an IBM OS/2 personal computer. Once the program runs, it may paint a window or perform some other function differently. This requires the programmer to make further changes. If the program is to be kept running on both platforms, the developer has to maintain two versions of the program. If the functionality of the program ever changes, the developer will need to make the changes in two places and test both versions. Dealing with the differences from platform to platform is a major problem for business application developers in companies with heterogeneous computing environments. Not only are applications effectively maintained twice, but the developer must learn the development rules for each platform.

Java technology addresses this problem through platform independence. If a developer writes a program in Java on a Sun/UNIX machine and then wants to use the same program on an IBM OS/2 PC, no changes in the application code need to be made. In fact, the program can be compiled and the executable version will run on either machine. Once executing, the program behaves the same on either machine. As of early 1998, Java technology still had some issues to resolve before it completely met the vision of platform independence, but it had gotten much closer to this vision than any other previous technology. Platform independence saves the time of maintaining multiple versions of a program, which can have a significant impact on a company with a heterogeneous computing environment.

19.2.6 Object-Oriented Programming

In the mid-1980s, object-oriented programming was declared the wave of the future. It was to revolutionize the way business application software developers programmed and to dramatically increase their productivity. After ten years, the predictions are far from being fulfilled. Very few large business systems projects are implemented with object technology, as opposed to a traditional procedural approach. Why has object-based development failed to achieve dominance? The answer lies in its complexity.

Object programming has historically been difficult to do well, especially on large projects. A key concept in object programming is that developers can build objects that are easily reused by other developers. The problem with this approach is that few people have consistent views on the granularity or level of detail required to implement object programming concepts, and effective coordination and sharing of code within a large group of developers is difficult. Software companies and researchers have tried to offer help in this area, but may have made the problem worse by providing complex features understood by only the best object programmers. Not only are the concepts difficult to understand and use, but even the names of the concepts are daunting: anachronism, polymorphism, and inheritance, for example.

Despite its complexity, object programming has good things to offer. The Java language has been designed as an object programming language that eliminates the most complex features and simplifies the most useful features. It remains difficult to create an effective large-scale object-based system, but the use of the Java language helps. With the approach the Java language takes, developers have the flexibility of object programming without many of the complexities found in C++.

19.2.7 Error Handling

The production program fails. The support team looks at the error message, which says only, "Error." The support team members must go through the code and try to determine what went wrong. The approach is a lengthy process, and it may take days to determine the cause and solution. The inevitable question is why the original developer did not do a better job of trapping errors and accurately documenting where such errors occurred. A large part of the long-term costs of maintaining applications would be eliminated if better information were made available to support personnel when an application has a problem.

The Java language addresses the challenge of error detection. Java technology implements a standard technique that catches errors as they occur (see Figure 19.1). Not only does the Java virtual machine provide a mechanism that detects errors as they occur, but it also indicates where they occurred. The error-catching mechanism in Java technology is a powerful way to watch for errors without having to check the results of every statement executed. This saves developers time by reducing the amount of error-checking code that has to be written while simultaneously increasing the level of error tracking. This capability of quickly and easily adding error handling reduces the coding time and debugging time of developers.

The downside of the Java approach to error handling is the time it takes to understand fully how it works. To developers comfortable with the C/C++/COBOL way of finding errors—by checking return codes—it is difficult to fully grasp the error-handling technique of Java technology. The Javas error-handling method will be new to almost all software developers. It will take them time to understand how it works and how to use it effectively. It is strongly believed by *via* World Network that Java technology's error handling was a strong contributor to the productivity and quality benefits they realized.

19.3 Aspects That Hinder Productivity

In general, developers coding in Java are more productive than developers coding in C or C++. There are, however, disadvantages to coding in Java and the following discussion focuses on three challenges that developers face.

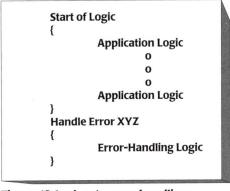

Figure 19.1   Java's error-handling approach

- Development tool immaturity

- Limited pool of experienced programmers

- Few examples of business systems

19.3.1 Development Tool Immaturity

The single most frustrating problem a Java developer faces is the lack of full-featured development tools. Developers using established languages such as C and C++ have enjoyed the advantages of advanced development tools that greatly simplify application building. Software companies have created productivity tools that have become commonplace in C, C++, and COBOL development. The Java language is new, and advanced development tools will take time to emerge. If a company decides to use Java in the 1990s, it must be prepared to take a step backward in software development tool capability.

19.3.2 Pool of Experienced Programmers

There is a limited base of Java developers to hire. A Zona Research study in mid-1997 suggested that roughly 40 percent of companies with more than 250 people had experimented with Java technology. Although the research suggested that within a year nearly all companies would have at least some experience with Java technology, this was the beginning sign of a shortage in Java skills. It will take several more years before Java experience is common among business systems developers, and therefore most development teams in the 1990s will not have significant internal or external experience from which to draw. Corporations will have to rely on their developers' ability to understand and learn the Java language quickly.

19.3.3 Few Examples of Business Systems

New projects look to other, more developed projects for advice and guidance in the use of a new technology. During the 1990s, Java technology is new, and examples of its use are limited. A project team deciding to use Java technology will have a more limited number of examples to leverage than they would have in a comparable C or C++ project.

Table 19.3 summarizes the developer productivity advantages and disadvantages of Java relative to C and C++ for building business applications.

**Table 19.3   Advantages and disadvantages
of Java versus C and C++**

Advantages	Disadvantages
No memory pointers	Development tools not mature
Better compiler	No pool of experienced programmers
Base classes	Few existing development sites
Programming easier systems	
Platform independence	
Simplified object programming	
Simplified error handling	

19.4   Java Reduces Application Development Time

Initially, there was concern when *via* World Network decided to use Java as its primary programming language. The key question was whether or not the development timeline would suffer as a result of choosing Java as the development language for a system that would contain more than 800,000 lines of code and measure more than 15,000 function points in application complexity. (The development timeline spanned a period of one year—from March 1996 through February 1997.) The following discussion examines the impact Java programming had on the productivity and quality of *via* World Network's first two production releases.

- Release One development

- Release One system testing

- Release One summary

- Release Two summary

- Production operations

19.4.1 Release One Development

via World Network's first release did in fact suffer a negative impact on its timeline as a result of the time required for the ramp-up of Java development. *via* World Network had to invest months of work setting up a development environment, creating coding standards, and learning how to create Java programs. This resulted in a slower start than if the C or C++ route had been taken. *via* World

Network was prepared for this delay in that it was viewed as an investment; but there was a concern about whether or not the investment would pay off once developers were past the ramp-up stage. The management expectation was that developers would be productive enough in the long run to compensate for the additional ramp-up time.

After the initial ramp-up of Java development, developers began to program business logic. It did not take long to see that the developers were productive in Java development; whether they were more or less productive than they would have been in C or C++ development was still to be determined.

Soon after development began, the *via* World Network development team faced an unexpected issue: no high-quality Java development tools existed. The project found itself without a graphical debugger and with an insufficient GUI painter. This affected the development team and took a toll on productivity. After six months, the emerging Java market provided developers with a sufficient toolset, but the damage to productivity had already been done.

For Release One (which lasted about six months), the team spent about 20 percent more time programming than was estimated for C or C++ development. There were several special considerations that had significant impacts on developer productivity during Release One.

- The infancy of the technology (*via* World Network began developing exclusively in Java in March of 1996)

- The lack of team knowledge of both Java and object programming

- The state of the development tools

- The lack of a preexisting application development environment

- The formation of a team of 100 people (technical support and application development) who had not previously worked together

19.4.2 Release One System Testing

When *via* World Network began system testing Release One and preparing for production rollout, it became evident that the developers were beginning to see advantages in Java technology over a C or C++ environment. This was largely attributable to the stability of the Java application code. C and C++ applications generally fail repeatedly during early testing as a result of memory management problems. This was not a problem with the Java applications, in which the logic was easy to read and debug and errors were easy to track down and resolve.

Two big problems were encountered at this phase that offset testing gains as the team prepared for production. The first difficult problem encountered was a memory leak. The memory leak was in the C code that was a necessary layer for accessing the database. Approximately 0.5 percent of Release One was built with C code used to access a database engine. In coding the C routines, a mistake had been made in the memory management routines, and had taken weeks to uncover. This loss of time offset much of the productivity gains realized during system testing.

The second big problem that arose during testing was that performance of the Java application did not meet expectations. The Java code was running ten to 20 times slower than similar C code. To speed up performance, development teams rewrote sections of code and sought creative ways to perform the same business logic. The time invested in performance was significant and offset the time savings the project had gained from productivity improvements in application testing. At the end of the system testing of Release One, via World Network had spent approximately four percent more time testing the system than would have been expected for a C or C++ system.

19.4.3 Release One Summary

In addition to the time spent in Release One for coding and system testing, the development team had a larger-than-normal overhead for initiating, supporting, and managing the application development. More than 8,000 days were spent in this area, of which two-thirds were accounted for by the creation of the execution architecture for *via* World Network (see Chapter 12). The 26 percent positive variance shown for this area is believed to have been attributable primarily to project management rather than to Java technology. Table 19.4 shows the overall time budgeted and actually spent by *via* World Network in creating its first production release.

Table 19.4   *via* **World Network Release One budgeted versus actual time**

Release One Area	Budgeted Days	Actual Days	Variance	Percent of Total
Application coding	2,307	2,781	−21%	23
Application testing	1,308	1,354	−4%	11
Administration supervision/ technical support	10,303	8,153	+21	66
Total effort	13,921	12,288	+12	−

Table 19.5   *via* **World Network Release Two budgeted versus actual time**

Release Two Area	Budgeted Days	Actual Days	Variance	Percent of Total
Application coding	3,836	3,502	+9%	37
Application testing	1,852	1,450	+22%	15
Administration supervision/ technical support	3,846	4,537	−18%	48
Total effort	9,534	9,489	0%	−

19.4.4 Release Two Summary

Release Two of *via* World Network's corporate travel management system was a much more stable development environment, because Java tools had matured, the team was more experienced, and the company's development processes were in place. The development of Release Two was significantly more productive than that of Release One, because significant benefits in coding and system testing productivity were realized (see Table 19.5). The application budget estimates for Release Two were again based on estimated guidelines for C/C++, and application coding exhibited a 9 percent gain in developer productivity while system testing saw a 22 percent productivity gain. The negative variance for administration/supervision/technical support was attributable to the following factors.

- Unanticipated execution architecture development

- Overestimation of gains in administrative/supervisory efficiency as the project moved into its second release

19.4.5 Production Operations

After even the first release, the benefits of Java technology became very clear as the production system ran much more smoothly during the first six months than a comparable C or C++ system conversion would have run. During the first six months of production, 75 percent fewer production defects were encountered than would have arisen over a comparable period in a C or C++ system. Significant time was saved during this phase, because developers were able to focus on building new applications rather than on fixing problems in the production application.

19.4.6 Overall Summary

Looking back on the life cycles of the first two releases of *via* World Network, developers in the first six months were less productive when coding in Java, but this was attributable more to the timing and nature of this first release than to the productivity of Java application development. As Release Two was developed, and the major issues declined in number, it was clear that Java developers were producing better code faster than they would have been in C or C++. It took the development team more time with the same number of people to build the more than 3,700 function points (or 200,000 lines of code) of Release One than to build the more than 11,300 function points (or 600,000 lines of code) of Release Two. As the environment stabilized and the tools matured, Java application developers were able to achieve substantial gains in productivity in Release Two compared with Release One. Developer productivity rose from 5.5 function points per month for Release One to 21.5 function points per month for Release Two (see Table 19.6).

19.5 Summary

Early users of Java programming (1996) were able to leverage Java technology's inherent productivity benefits to overcome delays resulting from the challenges associated with a new technology. As Java technology matures and as corporations become familiar with building Java systems, business development costs will decrease in comparison with C/C++ because the Java language promotes faster and better application development. Critical developer productivity considerations associated with Java applications are as follows.

Table 19.6 Comparison of *via* World Network Releases One and Two

Characteristic	Release One	Two
Lines of Java code	200,000.0	600,000.0
Lines of Java per function point	53.0	53.0
Function points	3,773.6	11,320.8
Total effort, days	12,288.0	9,488.6
Developer-days per month	18.0	18.0
Developer-months	682.7	527.1
Development days per function point	3.3	0.8
Function points per developer-month	5.5	21.5

- Programming is a complex and time-consuming task in which only incremental improvements in productivity have been made over the last few decades.

- Java simplifies the technology of programming, improves the quality of programming, and provides additional functions and features that reduce the amount of programming required. Java facilitates improvements in business application developer productivity in the following seven areas.
  - Memory management
  - Compiler
  - Base classes
  - Systems programming
  - Platform independence
  - Object programming
  - Error handling

- Three aspects of Java technology can hinder developer productivity: development tool immaturity, lack of experienced Java programmers, and scarcity of Java-based business systems.

- *via* World Network achieved application development productivity benefits over C/C++ through its use of the Java language. Companies may realize the same, better, or worse benefits depending on the skill-level makeup of the development team, the maturity of Java technology, and the quality/experience of the project management team.

- *via* World Network demonstrated significant gains in productivity between its first and second production releases. Measured in function points per developer-month, *via* World Network's development improved from 5.5 in Release One to 21.5 in Release Two.

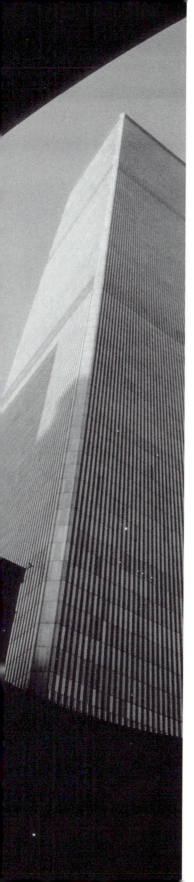

CHAPTER TWENTY

New Development Tools and Processes

20.1   Development Tools and Processes

Business application development projects lasting six or more months and having 20 or more developers require a well-planned and well-organized infrastructure. This infrastructure ensures that programmers will create applications that will operate consistently in production with acceptable maintenance costs.

To bring order to developmental chaos on large business systems, companies roll out standard development tools, build internal tools, and publish standards and processes for application developers to follow. If enforced, development tools and processes increase developer productivity and ensure that all pieces of a large application work together. This approach is not necessarily appropriate for small projects but is of paramount importance in building large business systems. Small development teams with short projects (less than six months) have a much easier time coordinating their work, because communication among team members is much simpler. Communication among the different teams and levels of management on a larger and longer project is complex, time-consuming, and often cumbersome. Small teams also require much less project infrastructure. They may not need sophisticated source code control mechanisms, strict coding standards, or even consistency in the development tools each person uses.

Obtaining, either through construction or purchase, the necessary tools and processes for a large development project is a common activity familiar to all experienced business systems developers. There is a wide range of tools used by application development teams. A list of the broad category of tools available would include:

• Office automation

• Project management

• Software development

• Maintenance engineering

• Quality assurance

• Testing

• Documentation

This chapter is not an exhaustive review of the overall application development tools and processes for Java programming. Instead, this chapter focuses on seven key tools of the overall development infrastructure. This chapter explores the impact of Java development on the seven critical areas in Table 20.1.

Table 20.1   Standard set of development tools and processes

Tool	Purpose
Program editor	Edit source files
Compilation tools	Compile applications
Debugger	Detect program errors
GUI painter	Create physical appearance of a GUI application
Coding standards	Instructions for developers on writing code
Source code control	Control changes in the application
Hardware and operating system	Platform on which system is to be developed and executed

20.2 Java Programming's Impact on Development

Development tools are crucial to the productivity of developers. Because these tools are closely tied to the underlying programming language, they increase developer productivity if the developers take the time to understand them thoroughly. In many cases, these tools are closely tied to a programming language, meaning that they are no longer viable with a different programming language. Once developers have dedicated time to learning current tools thoroughly and have used them extensively, it is a training and sometimes emotional challenge to replace them. Development tool replacement may also be a major financial hurdle for a business. Replacing application debuggers, GUI painters, and program editors is a significant undertaking.

20.2.1 Application Debuggers

An important development tool on large-scale software projects is the application debugger. An application debugger is a tool developers use to examine the execution of their program. It is a GUI tool that steps through each statement of a program and allows the developer to view or change program variables. This is a necessary tool for complex software development and saves developers significant time when tracking down problems. Because a powerful debugger helps developers create better applications, it also helps ensure a more robust final product. Figure 20.1 is an example screenshot of a debugger.

Debugging tools are created for a particular programming language. For example, a C debugger usually will not work with a COBOL application. Because the debugger steps through each line of code and has the ability to examine any variable, it is tied to the programming language.

When a business decides to develop in the Java language for the first time, they need to find a new debugger. Several Java debuggers are available, and they vary in quality. A new debugger requires significant investment to find, install, learn, and roll out to a development team of 20 or more developers.

The best source of information on existing Java debuggers is the Internet. A list of Java debuggers can be retrieved from the Internet and samples can be downloaded for examination. Before purchasing a new debugger, developers should test it. Once the debugger has been chosen, all developers will require some amount of training to use it effectively.

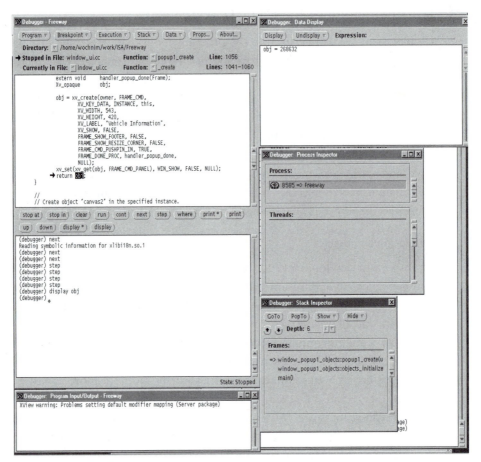

Figure 20.1   On-line debugger

20.2.2 GUI Painters

Programs that contain windows and graphical displays are commonly called GUI applications. A GUI application presents information to users graphically and allows them to use a keyboard or mouse to enter information and interact with the application (see Figure 20.2).

Creating large GUI applications is difficult and time-consuming. A GUI painter is a development tool that allows developers to use graphics to "paint a picture" of how the application is to look. The purpose of a GUI painter is to reduce significantly the effort required to build GUI applications. A good GUI painter allows a developer to create a picture of the application quickly, despite

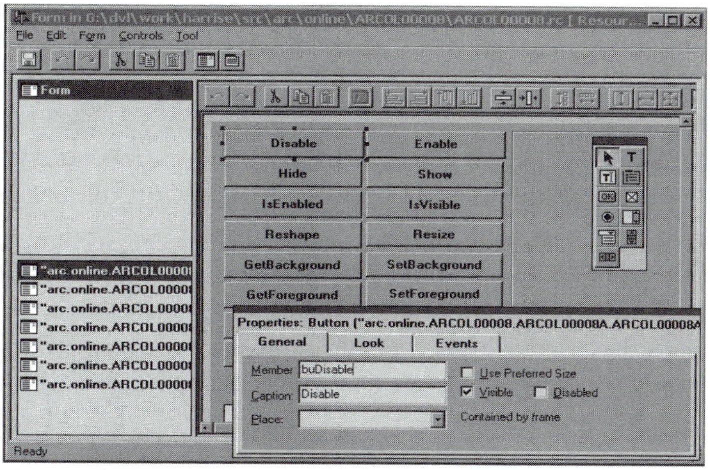

Figure 20.2   GUI painter

its complexity. It also allows users to see what the GUI application will look like before the developers spend time coding it.

Once the windows of the GUI application have been painted, the painter uses the information about the windows to generate much of the complex user interface code. Without a painter, GUI developers would be forced to code all of the commands manually to create and lay out every object on every window of an application. GUI painters usually generate more than 50 percent of the code required for a GUI application. Moreover, GUI painters retain the information about painted windows, making it easier for the developer to go back and make changes, reducing application maintenance time.

When a company begins to develop in the Java language, it requires a new painter. A non-Java painter will not produce Java code, nor is it able to leverage Java windowing features not available in many other programming languages (such as window layouts and imaging capabilities). Fortunately, learning painters is quite intuitive and does not require much training time.

As with debuggers, the best source of information on Java painters is the Internet. Most painters can be downloaded quickly and evaluated by members of the development team.

20.2.3 Program Editor

A program editor is the tool most commonly used on a software project. A program editor is used by developers to build their applications. Several editors are available, and the list continues to expand.

If developers are using an editor that is not specific to any language, the editor need not change. In the world of software development tools, editors are becoming more sophisticated, however. Editors today not only allow developers to edit code but also add features such as dynamic compilation, real-time syntax checking, and ties into debuggers for making quick fixes. For a program editor to support these advanced features, the editor must be tightly integrated with a particular programming language. Increasingly, these types of editors are being included in a software development package. It is common to purchase a debugger, painter, and editor as one package.

If the program editor that the project team was using prior to Java development was tightly integrated with a programming language, the project will have to replace it with either a language-independent editor or a Java editor. It is best to purchase a Java-specific editor if the project is forced to change, because it is likely to contain Java-specific features that will provide long-term developer productivity benefits.

20.2.4 Source Code Control Facility

A source code control facility is a tool or set of tools used to manage applications on a large project. It manages each source file by restricting access permissions and by making storing versions of the file. When developers are concurrently coding various applications, the project is open to source corruption if it does not effectively manage access to each source file. Situations can occur in which two developers attempt to change the same source file at the same time. At other times, changes in applications must be backed out because of improperly implemented changes. Source management tools address these issues.

Java applications create more source files and have stricter rules on the locations of files than comparable C, C++, and COBOL applications. In a large system, a company is faced with tighter management of an increasing number of source and executable files. Although the source code facility may continue to work with a large number of files, it should be tested early in the project to ensure that no problems are encountered midway into development. In most cases, the net impact of Java development is only minor updates in the existing source code control facility.

20.2.5 Compilation Utilities

Compiling an application requires a developer to have a compiler-read source code to create a runnable, executable program. The executable program is usually placed in a special location, allowing other developers to run the program.

The act of compiling a program is common for developers and occurs many times a day on development projects. Because of the importance and frequency of compiling, it is important for projects to supply tools to increase the reliability of compiling and decrease the required developer effort. Large-scale development projects require complex compilation tools to ensure that the appropriate files are compiled at the correct time with the right dependencies, and that the executables are placed in the proper locations.

Project developers wanting to improve the compilation process build tools that perform the housekeeping work when applications are compiled. These tools know where to locate the source files, how to compile them, where to place the executable programs, and what to clean up. Without a compilation tool, complete compilation of a single program could take a dozen commands. With a compilation tool, it takes only a single step to compile a program.

The steps these tools take to compile an application are relatively generic (language independent). The locations of the source files, where to place the executables, how to determine file dependencies, and other activities require only minor modifications for compiling Java programs. Because the steps in compiling Java programs are similar to those in compiling C, C++, and COBOL programs, the basic infrastructure of the compilation tools can be preserved. Rather than replacing the entire tool, it can be updated to reference the names of the new files, invoke the Java compiler, and account for any necessary changes in the directory structure. These types of changes in the compilation tools are not complex and do not change the overall approach a project has taken to compiling of applications.

20.2.6 Programming Standards

For large systems development projects, it is vital to have development processes and methodologies that describe how developers should design, code, test, and roll out applications. If rules are not put in place, projects will create applications that are difficult to maintain and support.

The most common examples of development standards are the programming rules enforced on a project. Large development teams establish programming standards early in the process before application development begins. Programming standards simplify future application enhancements and the support of applications in production.

The best approach to establishing Java coding standards is first to achieve a full understanding of the Java programming language. After one understands how to program in the Java language, a new set of programming standards for

Java development can be created by referencing the old set. If the project formerly had standards for C or C++, the translation is simple. If the project team previously used COBOL, updating the coding standards is more complex.

20.2.7 Development Platforms

At the beginning of a development project, the first major technical decision is choosing the hardware and operating system that will be used by application developers. This is a critical decision, because the development platform is much more expensive than any of the development tools or processes. Once the development platform has been chosen, all subsequent application development tool decisions must take into account the hardware and operating system that the developers will be using.

Java technology does not play a central role in the decision of which hardware or operating system is best for the project. Java's platform independence allows it to run on a wide variety of computers. Whereas Java programs are platform independent and do not impact the choice of development platform, the same cannot be said of application development tools. Many of these tools are not built with the Java language and are not platform independent. The project team's development platform decision should consider the availability of Java tools on that platform.

20.3 Switching to Java

via World Network is a good example of a company that changed its development tools and processes as a result of building Java-based systems. Even though application development was underway, *via* World Network made the switch to Java.

20.3.1 Development and Production Platform

Prior to making the decision to develop in Java, the project team had already decided on a platform for application development and production operations. Application developers were working on Intel personal computers running Windows NT and Windows 95. These developers were creating an Internet-based system in which a client application would execute on a personal computer and access travel reservation functionality executing on a Sun Microsystems platform. The back-end processing of the system was to be written in C or C++, and the GUI applications were to be programmed in Sybase's Power-Builder. Oracle had been selected as the database vendor. The development team had also begun to solidify the development processes and programming standards that would be used.

Before application programming began but after these technology decisions had been made, *via* World Network decided to change directions and build their travel reservations system in the Java language. Owing to Java technology's platform independence, no changes in the development hardware already purchased were necessary. However, many of the development tools, processes, and methodologies were modified or replaced.

20.3.2 Development Process and Methodology

When *via* World Network decided to use the Java programming language, the existing development processes and methodologies (which tell developers how to design, code, and test applications) had to be updated. The programming standards were rewritten to incorporate the Java syntax, but this was easy because the Java syntax is very similar to that of C and C++. Changing the programming standards took less than ten hours of work.

20.3.3 Source Code Control Facility

Prior to making the decision to use Java technology, *via* World Network had already installed a source code control facility. The facility used on the project was a combination of internally built tools and the Source Code Control System (SCCS), which is a standard feature within most vendors' versions of UNIX. The internally constructed tools comprised more than 100 programs that used a database to inventory and control every source file in the system. File permissions and the archiving of source revisions were handled by the SCCS tool. When *via* World Network made the decision to use the Java language, the only changes that had to be made in the source code control facility were to update the naming standards of the files and to account for minor directory structure changes. Both of these changes required only minor effort and took one person about 40 hours to complete.

20.3.4 Compilation Utility

A more difficult task for the team was to incorporate a compilation utility for Java applications into the development toolset. The project had previously used a UNIX utility (called "Make") to control the compilation of C and C++ applications. Although this utility would work with Java applications, the challenge was to create an infrastructure that would support the long-term application development of more than 50 people creating and updating more than 100,000 files.

The large number of files required tools to be written to supplement the compilation utility. The Java language also dictated a new organization scheme for applications as well as for adding new steps in the compilation process.

The objective was to create a simple, coordinated compilation tool that would require only a single command to execute and yet would support a wide variety of application development requirements. After a few weeks' effort, the work was completed. The tool successfully combined several complex compilation steps, requiring the developer to type only a single command. Listed below are the compilation steps automatically performed by the tool.

- Determine which Java source files were to be compiled.

- Determine the order in which the source files should be compiled.

- Determine the dependencies of each source file.

- Check each source file for compliance with programming standards.

- Compile each source file into an executable file.

- Move the newly created executables to the proper directory.

- Clean up temporary files.

One disadvantage discovered was that the compilation utility used by the project was originally designed to work with more common languages such as C and C++. The "Make" utility incorporates special rules and syntax that make compilation easier and faster for projects building C or C++ applications.

20.3.5 Program Editors

via World Network chose the program editors before the Java language was introduced (for example, vi, textedit, and emacs). None of these editors was tied to a particular language, and therefore developers did not have to change the editors they were using.

20.3.6 Debugger

Before joining *via* World Network, many of the team members had already been exposed to Sun Microsystem's "dbxtool" debugger. The dbxtool debugger is an easy-to-use graphical interface for Sun/UNIX platforms that was heavily relied on for debugging of C programs in previous projects. When the switch to Java programming was made, a new tool was required.

via World Network's first year of Java development (1996) came before tool manufacturers had had a chance to create good debugging tools. The project was forced to go without a graphical debugger, which increased application development time. Even after one year of Java development (early 1997), Java debugging tools were still not at the level of quality and functionality found in C and C++ environments.

20.3.7 GUI Painter

For *via* World Network, the Java GUI painter market matured much faster than the Java debugger market. The project team chose a powerful tool, Visual Café from Symantec. Symantec's GUI painter was furthest along in functionality and was relatively inexpensive, but it did not contain all of the functionality required by the project. To provide additional functionality, the technical team built standards and tools to generate program logic for objects such as images, audio, and window layouts. Once this additional work had been completed, developers could quickly paint, code, and execute GUI applications.

20.4 Summary

Many companies have significant investments in development tools and processes. A decision to create Java programs affects existing application development infrastructures. Some tools can be replaced, whereas most have to be updated. Table 20.2 summarizes the impact of Java on development tools and processes.

The key considerations regarding Java Technology's impact on development tools and processes are as follows.

Table 20.2   Java technology's impact on development tools and processes

Tool Process	Must Replace	May Replace	Must Change	Little or No Impact
Program editor		✔		
Compilation tools			✔	
Debugger	✔			
GUI painter	✔			
Programming standards			✔	
Source code control			✔	
Hardware and operating system				✔

- Of the many categories of tools used by application development projects, the seven categories that impact application developers are the ones listed in Table 20.2.

- Most companies moving to Java development are required to select, purchase, and install a new debugger and GUI painter.

- Most companies are required to make modifications in existing compilation tools, programming standards, and source code control facilities in order to support Java development.

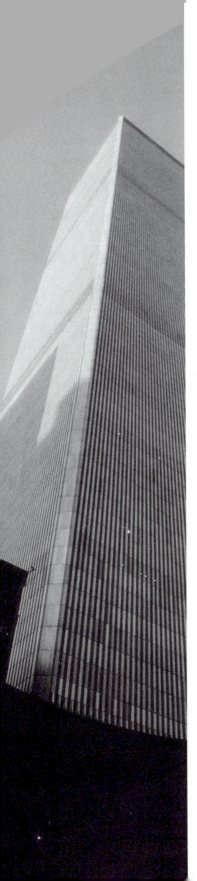

Glossary

ActiveX: A set of technologies and standards provided by Microsoft for interaction of applications over a network. A standard competing with the CORBA standard developed by the Object Management Group.

ANSI-C: A United States standard implementation of the C programming language.

API: *See Application Programming Interface.*

Application Programming Interface: Entry point into an application. One application can call another application through an API.

applet: A Java program that executes on a user's machine and performs some form of GUI interaction with the user. Typically, an applet is dynamically downloaded by a browser from a Web site at the time an appropriate Web page is accessed.

artificial intelligence: Use of computer technology for "artificial" mimicking of the human thought process, typically associated with the use of computer technology to solve complex problems.

Abstract Window Toolkit: The part of the Java language dealing with the presentation of information to a user. This portion of the Java language contains building blocks with which a developer can create Java GUI applications.

AWT: *See Abstract Window Toolkit.*

browser: An application executing on a user's machine that allows access to Internet- and intranet-based applications. Common commercial browsers are created by Microsoft and Netscape.

bug: An error or mistake in a program.

CGI: *See Common Gateway Interface.*

Common Gateway Interface: A scripting tool used by Web servers to execute commands. A network request received by a Web server may execute a CGI script to fulfill a request by a user.

client/server: A type of computing approach by which the applications are spread across multiple machines on the network. Client applications (typically performing user interface functions) execute on a user's device and communicate with applications and data stored in different parts of the network (typically on a server).

compiler: A tool used by developers that turns a text file of program statements into an executable program or binary file.

Common Object Request Broker Architecture. A common, standardized methodology by which applications interact over a network. The CORBA standard is dictated by a standards body, the Object Management Group (OMG).

CORBA: See Common Object Request Broker Architecture.

database: A storage repository for electronic data where data is stored in multiple tables or files. The sets of data in the different tables are "related" to each other by use of key data fields.

debugger: A tool used by software developers to find problems in applications. The debugger is a tool (typically a graphical tool) that allows a developer to watch the step-by-step execution of a program and view and modify variables in order to detect problems.

debugging: The act of using a debugger to find problems in an application.

decryption: The process of converting coded information from a secure, unreadable form into readable, usable content.

digital assistant: See Personal Digital Assistant (PDA).

Digital Expresso: A WWW site focusing on Java newsgroups.

dynamic download: The ability to transfer a Java program across the Internet to a user's machine and then execute it without having to compile it. This allows users to execute applications over a public network without having to perform and install them on their local machines.

EDI: See Electronic Data Interchange.

Electronic Data Interchange: A set of standards developed to assist the on-line transfer of data between two computer systems.

electronic commerce: Also called e-commerce. Business transactions occurring over a network, either public or private.

encryption: Conversion of data from a usable form to a form that no one can understand or use. Used for security purposes.

execution architecture: A layer of technology products and software that insulates business logic from the underlying technology. Used primarily by companies building large or multiple systems.

firewall: A system that filters network communications. A firewall is intended to keep unwanted and unauthorized network traffic from a public network (such as the Internet) out of an internal company network.

function point: A method of calculating the relative complexity of an application independent of the programming language. This tool has gained favor as a superior metric over the use of lines of code for measuring the development productivity of projects using different programming languages (programming languages vary in the relative amount of work performed "per line of code").

Gamelan: A WWW site containing several Java applications and applets.

gateway: A computer acting as a bridge between two different platforms or systems. It generally serves to interpret between two dissimilar network communication protocols.

green field project: A new project that can start with a clean slate regarding all technology decisions. The advantage of a green field project over a project-in-progress is that past decisions and/or implementations do not have to be reevaluated and/or redesigned with the use of a new technology.

Graphical User Interface: Applications executing on a user's machine that employ graphical techniques to retrieve and display information for the user

GUI: *See Graphical User Interface.*

HTML: *See HyperText Markup Language.*

HTTP: *See HyperText Transfer Protocol.*

HyperText Markup Language: A scripting language used to create applications that execute through browsers. These applications present information to and collect information from a user.

HyperText Transfer Protocol: The primary protocol (or standard) used to communicate over the Internet (or intranet).

Internet: Global, public network based on the TCP/IP protocol. This network was originally intended to serve the needs of the U.S. government and academic institutions.

intranet: Private network internal to a company leveraging the technologies used by the Internet.

JavaBeans: A Java programming feature that allows different applications and parts of applications to communicate with each other in a standard way. JavaBeans simplifies the communication between application components.

JavaScript: A scripting programming language with syntax similar to the Java language. JavaScript is used within Web pages to provide HTML with more interactive behavior.

JavaSoft: A division of Sun Microsystems responsible for maintaining the Java language and specifications.

Java DataBase Classes: Set of Java routines for accessing a database. These classes attempt to standardize database access for Java applications.

JDBC: *See Java DataBase Classes.*

Java Development Kit: The basic tools necessary to write and run Java applications. Included in the JDK is a set of class libraries, a compiler, and a virtual machine on which to execute Java applications.

JDK: *See Java Development Kit.*

JIT compiler: *See Just-in-time compiler.*

Just-in-time compiler: A compiler that compiles a program at the time it is run. A static compiler, or simply a compiler, compiles a program prior to runtime.

kiosk: A user interface device used for self-service applications. An example of a kiosk is an ATM machine.

LAN: *See Local Area Network.*

Local Area Network: A network internal to a company typically spanning a small area; a collection of user machines within a building, for example.

legacy systems: Existing, older systems that a company already has installed. Generally these systems are associated with IBM mainframe technology.

library: A programming technique whereby routines are packaged together and made available to other programs. This allows multiple programs to share a single set of code for complex operations such as network communications or database access.

Make: A compilation utility for developers found on UNIX systems.

memory fault: A program error whereby the application places information in memory that corrupts other data or corrupts the application itself.

methodology: Processes, procedures, and standards for performing a particular application development task.

metrics: A measurement tool for monitoring the state of an application system or process. Metrics might include failure rate or programmer productivity.

multimedia: A variety of human interfaces with a computer system, such as image display and manipulation, touch screen technology, and sound and voice response/recognition.

multithreading: A programming technique that allows a single program to create multiple instances of itself and execute the same logic concurrently. Used primarily to reduce the elapsed time of overall processing by breaking the problem into similar components and processing all components concurrently.

network computer: A desktop computer without any local disk. It accesses all of its information over the network.

Object Management Group: Standards body that defines the CORBA standard.

object-oriented technique: A programming technique whereby code is grouped into objects. Each object has application logic and data. Object technology was designed to reduce application maintenance costs and increase the reusability of application logic.

OMG: *See Object Management Group.*

operating system: A large program that controls a computer. All other programs run on top of an operating system. Example operating systems include UNIX, Windows 95, and Windows NT.

OS/2: An operating system created by IBM. Used on both desktop computers and servers.

packages: Collections of Java source code files. Packages help to organize Java code for large applications.

painter: Also called GUI painter. A development tool used to create GUI applications.

Personal Digital Assistant: PDA. A small electronic device used for organizing personal functions.

platform independence: The ability to execute the same file unchanged on a variety of hardware/operating system platforms.

plug-in: An application or part of an application that can easily be added to or "plugged" into another application. An example is an image display application that is added to another GUI application such as a browser.

port: To move an application from one hardware/operating system platform to another.

procedural programming: A programming technique whereby statements are executed in a sequential manner. Sequences of statements are grouped together into what are called functions. Functions call other functions in a sequential manner.

protocol: A term generally used to describe a network communication standard.

prototype: A test or scaled-back version of an application that mimics a fully functional application. It gives users a sense of what the real application will do and look like once it is complete.

RDBMS: *See Relational DataBase Management System.*

Relational DataBase Management System: A database in which data is stored in multiple tables related by key fields.

scalability: The ability of a system to grow as the transaction volume increases over time.

SCCS: *See Source Code Control System.*

Source Code Control System: A source code control utility on UNIX-based systems.

Secure Socket Layer: Standard secure protocol for communicating over the Internet. It was created to help address security issues regarding Internet communication.

shell: A program source file containing the start of a program. A shell is used to give developers a start on their applications and help ensure consistency across multiple applications.

Solaris: Operating system for Sun Microsystems computers. Solaris is a Sun-specific version of UNIX.

Source code control: Tools used to control the source code of applications. These tools typically take care of access control, version control, and archiving.

SSL: *See Secure Socket Layer.*

TCP/IP: Family of protocols for communicating over networks. This is the network protocol family used by the Internet.

threading (or **threaded**): A term used to describe a program that executes multiple streams of commands simultaneously. Used primarily for performance reasons. Each stream of a program is called a thread.

Three-tier system: A system that has a user interface, server-side processing, and a data repository. The user interface is considered tier one, the server-side processing is considered tier two, and the data repository is considered tier three.

time-out: Occurs when a program makes a call to another program and does not receive a response. After a certain amount of time, the calling program "times-out," assuming that the called program will not respond, and either produces an error message or continues processing.

two-tier system: A system that has a user interface and data repository. The user interface is considered tier one and the data repository is considered tier two.

UNIX: Class of operating systems that are generally considered "open." Examples of UNIX operating systems are Sun Solaris and HP-UX.

user interface: That portion of a system with which end-users see and interact. Examples include GUI applications, kiosks, PDA's and voice response/recognition.

virtual machine: A platform-specific program that executes Java programs. There is a virtual machine for each platform on which Java programs can run, including both operating systems and browsers.

virus: A class of programs developed to infect other programs or platforms. Viruses generally exploit weaknesses in applications or systems and are intended to perform some sort of mischief ranging from a message display to actual vandalism.

Web page: A page of information available over the WWW. These pages are built through the use of HTML.

Web server: A program used by companies to let users access information over the Internet or intranet. A Web server receives and responds to messages from browsers and other devices that use the HTTP network protocol.

widget: An item on a GUI application, such as a button, scroll list, or image.

World Wide Web, or simply the Web: Information and services provided over the Internet using the HTML and HTTP standards.

WWW: *See World Wide Web.*

Index

Mission-Critical Java™ Project Management

Addison-Wesley Information Technology Series

Capers Jones, Series Editor

The information technology (IT) industry is in the public eye now more than ever before because of a number of major issues in which software technology and national policies are closely related. As the use of software expands, there is a continuing need for business and software professionals to stay current with the state of the art in software methodologies and technologies. The goal of the Addison-Wesley Information Technology Series is to cover any and all topics that affect the IT community: These books illustrate and explore how information technology can be aligned with business practices to achieve business goals and support business imperatives. Addison-Wesley has created this innovative series to empower you with the benefits of the industry experts' experience.

For more information point your browser to
http://www.awl.com/cseng/series/it/

Gregory C. Dennis and James R. Rubin, *Mission-Critical Java™ Project Management: Business Strategies, Applications, and Development.* ISBN: 0-201-32573-X.

Capers Jones, *The Year 2000 Software Problem: Quantifying the Costs and Assessing the Consequences.* ISBN: 0-201-30964-5.

Sergio Lozinsky, *Enterprise-Wide Software Solutions: Integration Strategies and Practices.* ISBN: 0-201-30971-8.